RIDERS OF THE WINDS
The Story of Ballooning

DON DWIGGINS

This dramatically illustrated history of ballooning covers the full span of achievement from the early experiments of the Montgolfiers in 1783 up to the present. The reader embarks on a thrilling adventure as he rides the often fickle and treacherous winds with some of the greatest, most daring balloonists of all time—Pilatre de Rozier, Jean-Pierre Blanchard, Madame Thible, Etienne Gaspard Robertson, Charles Ritchel, John Wise, Monck Mason, Jean and Jeannette Piccard, and Captain W. Kittinger, Jr.—to name just a few.

In this comprehensive account Dwiggins not only explores ballooning as an adventurous sport but also describes the important scientific and military uses of balloons over almost two centuries. A concluding section on modern-day sport ballooning provides information on how and where to get ballooning instruction and practice.

Vivid first-hand accounts by some of the pioneers of ballooning, a wealth of fascinating facts and anecdotes illustrated with scores of historical prints and photographs make *Riders of the Winds* an engrossing reading experience.

RIDERS

OF THE WINDS

DON DWIGGINS's lifelong love of flying has
led him to intensive research into the
history of aeronautics. The result has
been scores of articles and books on the
subject, among them: *Bailout: The Story
of Parachuting & Skydiving; Barnstorm-
ers: Flying Daredevils of the Roaring
Twenties; Famous Flyers & the Ships
They Flew; Into the Unknown;* and *On
Silent Wings.*

A man of many talents, Dwiggins is
not only an award-winning writer but
also a licensed pilot, flight instructor,
photo journalist, and aviation editor. He
lives with his wife in Malibu, California.

RIDERS OF

THE STORY

OF BALLOONING

THE WINDS

by DON DWIGGINS

HAWTHORN BOOKS, INC.

Publishers/NEW YORK

RIDERS OF THE WINDS

Library of Congress Catalog Card Number: 73-371
ISBN: 0–8015–6378–X

3   4   5   6   7   8   9   10

CONTENTS

PREFACE

Since the beginnings of recorded history man has marveled at the mysteries of the sky, and been inspired by the ever-changing beauty of cloudland. Yet it has been barely two centuries since man first escaped the bonds of gravity and took his first faltering step toward exploration of space.

Today, man has been to the moon . . . sent robot spaceships to the distant planets . . . put amazing scientific satellites into earth orbit to study the weather, expand communications, and improve his environment by seeking sources of pollution.

All these space sciences have their origin in ballooning, which gave mankind a new perspective on his home planet. Today, through the resurgence of hot-air ballooning, we can once again enjoy the serenity of cloudland in a safe and exciting sport, one Marie Antoinette called the "Sport of the Gods."

ACKNOWLEDGMENTS

Riders of the Winds started out as something of a hobby in the 1930s, when the author undertook a search of United States Patent Office files for materials dealing with the origin and growth of aeronautics in America. The field was so fascinating that research expanded into a consuming study of source material in many of the nation's public and private libraries.

Correspondence with hundreds of inventors, balloonists, and others shaped an exciting story of our aeronautical heritage, and *Riders of the Winds* is that story. Through it runs the challenge of constantly new frontiers, and the determination of pioneer aeronauts to explore the farthest reaches of the sky.

Thanks are due the staffs of many libraries, including the American Philosophical Society Library, American Imprints Inventory, American Historical Association, Mrs. Henry L. Brownback Collection, Chicago Historical Society, Crerar Library, Franklin Institute, Historical Society of Delaware, Historical Society of Pennsylvania, Henry E. Huntington Library, Institute of the Aeronautical Sciences, National Archives, National Air and Space Museum, Smithsonian Institution, and Library of Congress.

Among the hundreds of individuals who helped this book come into being, special thanks go to Bill Berry, Preston Bassett, Dave Burt, Bruce Comstock, editor of

Ballooning Journal, Jim Knight of Balloon Ascensions, Ltd., Vincent E. Lally, GHOST program manager, Larry J. Manderscheid of Raven Industries, Inc., Don Piccard and Wilma Piccard, Ernest Robischon of the National Air and Space Museum, George Stokes, Bob Waligunda of Balloon Enterprises, Inc., and Ed Yost of Dakota Industries. And finally, to Carolyn Trager, my editor, who put her faith wholeheartedly behind the project.

RIDERS
OF THE WINDS

1

SPORT OF
THE GODS

The bulging shadow of our black hot-air balloon, *Tar Baby*, slithers silently across the unfolding landscape, less than a hundred feet below our wandering wicker basket, startling dogs and chickens and sometimes people. The ghostly silence of our drifting flight is broken by barks, cackles, and shouted greetings.

Beside me is tall, lanky Don Piccard, of the famous aeronaut family. He prefers ground-skimming to the stratospheric jaunts of his parents, Jean and Jeannette Piccard. "Kissing through grain fields, bounding up through treetops, then down into the next field to flirt with flowers—this is the freedom of the Montgolfier!" he exclaims.

What an experience, I thought! Here we were, sailing across Perris, California, almost two hundred years since the first Montgolfier hot-air balloon sailed across Paris,

Don Piccard's hot-air balloon *Tar Baby*

France! Marie Antoinette called it the "Sport of the Gods," a phrase that describes the sense of aristocratic aloofness, the aura of detachment one experiences in this delightful sport.

The revival of hot-air ballooning in recent years has given us a sport enjoyed today by hundreds of men and women, who find spiritual as well as physical uplift in silent flight. You don't go *up* in a balloon—you remain still, as the world floats silently away from you.

"Micro-meteorology is a wonderful thing," Piccard is saying. "Put a glider pilot in a free balloon and his eyes open wide; he sees things he never noticed before!" Wisps of vapor become meaningful signals to the trained balloonist. Piccard points a bony finger ahead, eyes keen, alert. A tiny dust devil dances a dervish and disappears.

"In fourteen seconds we go thataway," he says.

I watch our shadow flow across a ravine and up the far slope, and in just fourteen seconds it stops, pirouettes, moves off at a tangent.

"A mini-front," Piccard explains. "This is unstable air. We either ride up over it, or sit it out here."

Above, towering thunderheads mark heavy thermal action, giant cauliflowers laced with lightning. To go up and over the area of instability means risking a fast trip up a hot convective chimney. Better to land. Piccard opens the valve of our propane burner. A blowtorch flame blazes inside the nylon balloon, with a thunderous roar. We leapfrog a rock pile, I imagine the way Apollo 11 Comdr. Neil Armstrong guided Eagle to a soft moon landing.

Startled dogs bark, a horse rears, neighing in alarm, a frightened cottontail dives for cover. Piccard skillfully controls our descent, until our basket slams against a huge boulder. He jerks the rip-panel line, and *Tar Baby* splits open, top to bottom, writhing in undulating death throes.

Two ranchers run up to help us roll up the balloon and stuff it into the three-by-three-by-four-foot basket. "Man, what a way to round up cows!" one yells. In a moment up drives Mrs. Don Piccard, in the family jalopy, towing a small trailer, their personal balloonport. "Why don't you take up golf?" she sighs.

3

Two ranchers
help roll up
Piccard's balloon
after a rough
landing.

Balloon chasing has been a part of the sport since 1783. Besides chasing, there's other strenuous work. Balloonists are up early, before daybreak, to fly before the winds come.

Piccard carries a tripod of tent poles to hold open the balloon's mouth, the rest of the bag stretched out downwind. The wicker basket is placed on its side, load lines attached, propane tanks and burner placed in position. The burner is lighted and its flame directed toward the open neck, sending hot air rushing inside. Slowly the big

4

bag trembles, rises, fills out. It tugs at the lines, ready to be off.

Passengers swing aboard, wearing crash helmets. Instrument cases are added—one for flight, with compass, rate-of-climb indicator, and altimeter, the other a short-wave radio, to keep in touch with the ground crew. Then it happens—you glance down and all at once the world is far below you! Up here all is stillness, broken only by the song of a distant meadowlark.

Until recently, ballooning has been a rich man's sport.

Prior to the revival of hot-air ballooning, the cost of lifting-gas was exhorbitant. A single flight with helium, hydrogen, or coal gas costs upward of $150, compared to as little as $2.50 an hour for propane gas, the source of heat for the hot-air balloon, which goes up because its total gross weight—balloon, basket, passengers, even the air inside and immediately outside the bag—is less than the atmospheric air it displaces. The higher you go the thinner the atmosphere becomes. When the densities become equal, you've reached your ceiling.

Over the years various means have been tried to steer balloons and give them lateral, or sideways, control, but in essence balloons are riders of the winds. They go where the winds blow. Skillful aeronauts can find the best winds, which may blow in half a dozen directions within a few hundred feet. Competition ballooning, therefore, involves a good knowledge of meteorology as well as aerostation, as ballooning is called. Awards are given for the longest, highest, and most enduring ascensions, but most exciting are Hare and Hounds races, which date back to the nineteenth century.

A typical Hare and Hounds race took place in July, 1909, at Hurlingham, near London, when a half dozen hydrogen-filled "hound" balloons set out after a "hare"— the balloon *Imp*, piloted by the Hon. C. S. Rolls. Three of the chase balloons were owned by women—Baroness von Heeckeren's *L'Esperance*, the Hon. Mrs. Assheton Harboard's *Valkyrie*, and Mrs. John Dunnville's *La Mascotte*. Rolls sailed his *Imp* across the heart of London, dipping to salute the cheering crowds, and came down near Wickford, in Essex. One by one the others sought favorable winds, and remarkably, one balloon, *Satellite*, flown by A. M. Singer, landed within a dozen yards of *Imp*.

Newspaper publisher James Gordon Bennett spurred

The start of a Hare and Hounds race at Hurlingham, England, in July 1909. At that time ballooning was a sport only the wealthy could afford because of the high cost of lifting-gas.

interest in sport ballooning by offering a handsome trophy to the winner of an annual race. The first, in 1906, was won by an American army officer, Lt. Frank P. Lahm, in the balloon *United States*. Lahm and a passenger, Maj. Henry B. Hersey, rose from Paris, crossed the English Channel by night, and came down at Whitby in Yorkshire, England covering 410 miles in twenty-two hours seventeen minutes.

A Belgian balloonist, Ernest Demuyter, won the James Gordon Bennett Trophy three times in succession, from 1922 to 1924, retiring the cup. Belgium offered a new prize, and the races continued. Demuyter won six races

7

in all, evidence that skill, not luck, is important in balloon racing.

The revival of hot-air ballooning after World War II marked the birth of a new era of aerostation—for less than the price of a $5,000 sports car, one could purchase a fine new balloon complete with bag, car, propane heater, and crash helmets for the passengers.

If any one man was responsible for the rebirth of hot-air ballooning, it was Ed Yost, of Sioux Falls, South Dakota. Yost was working at General Mills, Inc., in the 1950s, when the Navy's Skyhook program started to send instrumented balloons into the stratosphere for cosmic ray studies. What they needed was a balloon of tough, lightweight material.

General Mills had technical experience making cellophane food wrappers, which led to their government contract to build a giant polyethylene balloon for stratospheric research. They also developed smaller training balloons that could be inflated cheaply with hot air. Yost left General Mills and with three others started Raven Industries at Sioux Falls, continuing government work on laminated mylar/nylon balloons. Today Raven is the world's largest hot-air balloon maker.

In 1955 Yost and his wife built a thirty-nine-foot diameter polyethylene balloon in their backyard. He designed a multiple-burner propane heater that inflated the bag with 37,500 cubic feet of hot air. It rose to the limit of its rope tether. After five more years of development work, Yost completed the first successful modern hot-air balloon, forty feet in diameter. Inflated with 30,000 cubic feet of hot air, it was made of mylar/nylon laminate, and had a lifting power of 450 pounds. Yost ascended to 9,300 feet and came down three hours fifteen minutes later.

Don Piccard, who began ballooning with the United States Navy at Lakehurst, New Jersey, at the outset of World War II, made his first ascent in 1933 with his mother, Jeannette Piccard. After the war he modified an unmanned Japanese Fugo war balloon, adding a Davies mine lamp valve and rip panel, and developed a system of side inflation from hydrogen bottles still in use today. He added a kapok-lined aluminum basket and drag rope, and on February 16, 1947, made the first postwar ascension in the United States, from the Minneapolis parade grounds. The flight lasted just over two hours.

Next he bought a war surplus rubberized Navy balloon for $10, and flew it half a dozen times over Pennsylvania, using coal gas and natural gas. Piccard met Gilmore T. Schjeldahl, a veteran balloon-maker of Northfield, Minnesota, and worked on balloon research there for four years, before being recalled to active duty with the Navy in 1950 as a balloon instructor.

In 1954 Piccard acquired a dozen war surplus training balloons and formed the Balloon Club of America. It eventually merged with the Wingfoot Lighter Than Air Club of Akron, to become the Balloon Federation of America. Today BFA is sanctioned by the National Aeronautic Association and the Federation Aeronautique Internationale, as the official representative for sport ballooning in America.

BFA represents more than 300 active aeronauts flying an estimated two hundred balloons. Of these about half are Ravens, one third Piccards, and the rest produced by smaller firms or individuals. Piccard manufactures about fifty balloons a year at Newport Beach, California, and recently established a new base at Ballymurray House, Ireland, to build sport balloons there for the European Common Market. Piccard, who once worked at Raven,

Raven balloons—"the most beautiful balloons in the world"

considers their balloons among the best flying today—
Raven advertises them as *The Most Beautiful Balloons
In The World*. Piccard's propane burner is manufactured
under a licensing agreement with Raven. Piccard balloons
are designed for both aesthetic beauty and rough usage,
of coated nylon sewn with double-needle lockstitch, the
load tapes reinforced with a third row of stitching. They
retain the traditional wicker basket.

On July 19, 1961, Piccard rose 34,462 feet above sea
level in a plastic balloon, the *Golden Bear*, and came
down seventy-five minutes later with five world records.
The flight, from Faribault, Minnesota, ended at dusk. "In

the hastening gloom," he recalled, "I chose a grove of trees for my landing. I drifted to the top of a tree, tied my craft to the branches and continued deflating my balloon. The chase car arrived shortly and we packed the balloon and gear and called it a day."

Hot-air balloons are designated AX, to differentiate them from Class A gas balloons. They are further grouped into subclasses according to size, from AX-1 to AX-10. A hot-air distance record of 196.71 miles, was set March 29, 1972, by balloonist Matt Wiederkehr from St.

Don Piccard adjusts the multiple burner propane heater in one of his new wicker baskets.

Ground skimming in a hot-air balloon is a lovely way to see the countryside.

Paul, Minnesota. He set a duration record of eight hours forty-eight minutes at the same time.

An official hot-air altitude record was set June 12, 1971, by Chauncey Dunn, who rose to 32,949 feet above sea level over Longmont, Colorado. One year later, on July 14, 1972, Julian Mott, a British balloonist, claimed a new record of 36,000 feet.

An amazing unofficial record was set in 1966, when Tracy Barnes made the first coast-to-coast flight in a hot-air balloon. His five-month adventure began at Coronado, California, and ended at Atlantic City, New Jersey. Barnes had his share of excitement—he crashed into a mountain peak 100 miles east of San Diego . . . got lost in the Rockies . . . landed in the bottom of the Grand Canyon . . . snagged a bridge and was dumped into the Allegheny River.

For most people, hot-air ballooning is simply a lovely way to get away from it all, drifting silently under a bubble of warm air, wherever the winds blow.

At the end of this book, you will read how to become a balloonist, where to learn the art, where to buy a balloon, and how to maneuver one. It's a whole new adventure, just waiting for you!

2

WHAT GOOD
IS A
NEWBORN
BABE?

Looking backward across two centuries, to the very beginnings of ballooning, it's hard to imagine how casually it all came about, how slowly people recognized the tremendous impact conquest of the sky would have on the course of history. At first, the frail little bubbles of hot air and hydrogen gas were simply a form of amusement, until leading scientists began to realize what an amazing thing they had unleashed. News traveled slowly in the late eighteenth century, by horse and carriage and by sailing vessels—how great it would be, they mused, to send letters by balloon!

As an historical event, the first manned balloon ascent two centuries ago was a scientific triumph comparable to the first heavier-than-air flights of the Wright brothers in 1903 and to Astronaut Neil Armstrong's first step upon the Moon in 1969.

Pilatre de Rozier, an energetic young chemist, appealed to King Louis XVI to support his project for the honor of France—surely a man of science was needed to handle the task! The king agreed, and on November 21, 1783, the stage was set for man's first escape from the bonds that had held him earthbound since the beginnings of time.

Five months had passed since Joseph and Etienne Montgolfier sent a paper balloon up 6,000 feet over the village of Annonay, on June 5, 1783. Benjamin Franklin, in France at the time, reported the balloon's total weight as 1578 lb. with a lifting force of 578 lb. The thirty-three-foot sphere was filled with smoke, from burning straw. It rose because the hot air inside the balloon was lighter than the air it displaced, just as a bubble of swamp gas rises to the surface of a pond.

Curiously, the Montgolfiers were not aware of the precise role played by hot air—they thought the balloon went up because of the smoke itself. In those days, scientists knew little about the elements; since medieval times they listed them as fire, air, earth, and water. When combustion took place, they believed, the "essence" of fire was driven off in the form of smoke—they called it *phlogiston*. So, it was phlogiston that made their paper bag ascend, the Montgolfiers assumed.

Another type of balloon attracted considerable interest in the year 1783—a sphere of varnished silk filled with hydrogen, then known to science as *inflammable air*. The first was a thirteen-foot sphere designed by

A drawing of the period shows the ascent of the Montgolfiers' balloon from Annonay, France, on June 5, 1783.

noted French physicist, Jacques Alexander César Charles. He filled it with inflammable air made by pouring 498 pounds of sulphuric acid over half a ton of iron filings.

During the reign of Louis XVI, last of France's monarchs, scholars like Monsieur Charles were favorites in court. At that time, the rise of the bourgeois middle-class, suppressed for more than a century by the monarchy, threatened the very existence of the ruling class. Hence, there was among the nobility a rage to learn that has been described as an intellectual fever.

The success of the two bourgeois inventors in the village of Annonay called for drastic action in Paris. Another favorite of the king, Bartholomy Faujas de Saint Fond, raised a public subscription to finance the Charles balloon, which was built of rubberized silk, by Anne-Jean and M. N. Robert. On the night of August 26, 1783, the Charles balloon, fully inflated after four days effort, was towed from Place des Victoires two miles to the Champ

Jacques Alexandre César Charles's hydrogen balloon aroused curiosity and excitement among Parisians when it was brought to the Champ de Mars on August 26, 1783.

de Mars, where there was more room for the launch. A Parisian paper reported: "Cab drivers on the road were so astonished they were impelled to stop their carriages and kneel humbly, hat in hand, whilst the procession passed."

Although it rained the next day, a huge crowd turned out. At 5 o'clock a cannon was fired and up went the Charles balloon more than half a mile before it vanished into the clouds. Among those present was Benjamin Franklin, United States minister to France, who was in Paris handling diplomatic relations to conclude the American Revolution.

Franklin's papers include a number of interesting comments on ballooning; to him it was more than a fad —it had a great future. When a bystander asked what possible good a balloon could be, Franklin shrugged: *"Eh, à quoi bien l'enfant qui vient de naître?"* (What good is a newborn babe?)

The day ended on a hilarious note, when the strange ball came down in a field, fifteen miles distant, a thing from space that utterly frightened a group of peasants. They attacked the ugly monster as it rolled and oozed across the ground, stabbing at it with pitchforks, then retreating from the awful stench of escaping gas, before it finally deflated. In anger, they tied the limp bag to the tail of a horse and whipped it into a gallop, ruining the world's first gas balloon.

Franklin divided his interest in the new art of ballooning with matters of state. France was eagerly awaiting settlement of the war with England in which she'd involved herself on behalf of American independence. One week after the Charles balloon ascension, treaties were

This engraving of a balloon with sail, rudder, and paddle wheels is among the Franklin Papers in the American Philosophical Society Library.

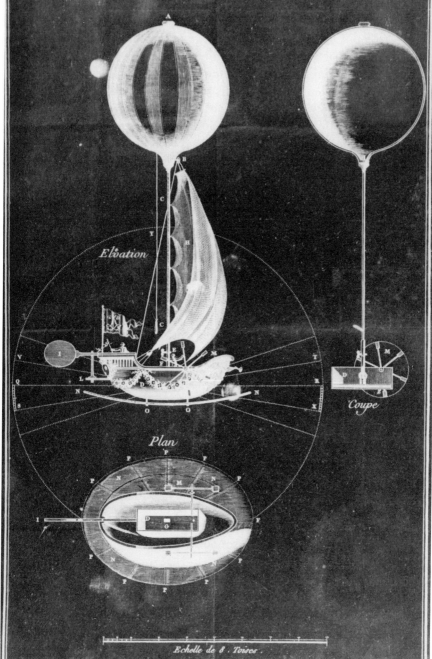

ESSAI SUR L'ART DE DIRIGER A VOLONTÉ LA CHALOUPE D.

Elevation

Plan

Coupe

Echelle de 8. Toises.

signed between the United States and England, and between England and France, and Franklin could relax. On August 30 he wrote to an old friend, Sir Joseph Banks of the Royal Society of London: "Some suppose flying to be now invented; since men may be supported in the air, nothing is wanted but some light, handy instruments to give and direct motion." Among his papers he left numerous fanciful schemes to make balloons navigable.

Franklin was confined to bed the following month when Etienne Montgolfier brought to Versailles a gaily painted balloon of waterproof linen, forty-six feet in diameter. It was inflated with phlogiston and sent up with the first living passengers to explore the sky—a sheep, a cock, and a duck. All became favorites in the Royal Menagerie.

By mid-October Rozier and Etienne Montgolfier completed the world's first man-carrying balloon. It stood seventy-four feet high and was elegantly painted with signs of the zodiac, fleur-de-lis, and, of course, the king's monogram. Beneath it hung a wicker promenade encircling a fire grate.

It was very impressive—high as a seven-story house, 1,600 pounds in weight, and filled to bursting with phlogiston. Rozier stepped aboard on the calm afternoon of October 15, 1783, stirred up the fire and signaled his ground crew to unwind the winch rope. The balloon rose smoothly to a height of 84 feet and hung there five minutes before Rozier shouted to be brought down. Smiling but pale, he accepted the congratulations of the crowd and was able to report finding nothing up there to worry about—no layers of poisonous gas some believed existed in the sky.

Rozier made two more practice solo ascents, each time balancing the wicker basket with a 100-pound weight on

Pilatre de Rozier made the first manned balloon ascent on October 15, 1783.

the opposite side. Then, on November 21, Rozier invited a friend, Monsieur Girond de Villette, to replace the sand bag. They ascended more than 3,000 feet and stayed aloft nine minutes, enjoying the view. Villette, incidentally, has been forgotten in history because of what happened next, but to him should go the honor of being the world's second aeronaut.

Immediately after descending, more straw was heaped on the fire and Villette's place was taken by an infantry major, the Marquis d'Arlandes. A hush fell over the crowd assembled at the launch site, the garden of the royal palace at La Muette, in the Bois de Boulogne. At 1:54 P.M. the rope was cut and away sailed the world's first free balloonists, higher than the treetops, higher than the church steeples, vanishing in the distance, driven by a brisk northwest wind across the Seine River, above the very heart of Paris.

As the balloon began to settle, Rozier cried to Monsieur d'Arlandes in alarm, "Look, there is the river! We're going down! Let us increase the fire!"

Quickly they tossed more straw onto the flames, which blazed upward furiously; sparks began burning numerous holes in the bag. Two ropes of the net snapped. Rozier grabbed a wet sponge and hurriedly put out the spot fires. Safely beyond the city rooftops, once more they descended, this time landing more than five miles distant.

Franklin still wasn't impressed. He wrote to his friend Sir Joseph: "These machines must always be subject to be driven by the winds. Perhaps mechanic art may find easy means to give them progressive motion in a calm, and to slant them a little into the wind." He added a postcript that would become a footnote to history: "It is supposed that balloons may be sufficient for certain purposes, such as elevating an engineer to take a view of an enemy's army, works, etc., conveying intelligence into or out of a besieged town, giving signals to distant places, or the like." Eighty-six years later, Paris would depend on balloons for communication with the outside world, while under siege during the Franco-Prussian War.

Franklin was also a witness to the first human ascent in a hydrogen balloon on December 1, 1783, when he stationed his carriage downwind from the Tuilleries to watch Monsieur Charles and M. N. Robert sail away in a balloon 27½ feet in diameter, coated with a rubbery substance called *caoutchouc* and pronounced like a sneeze. Etienne Montgolfier first launched a small signal balloon to check the wind, then the two aeronauts climbed aboard a pretty wicker boat, tossed over a bag of sand and up they went.

Charles's balloon was the first to include such things as a valve at the top for releasing gas to start a descent; ballast bags of sand; a barometer for measuring height; and impregnated silk. The only balloon devices he hadn't thought of were the rip panel, invented by John Wise, an American aeronaut, and the drag rope, first used by Charles Green, an Englishman. Gas balloons quickly became known as *Charlières*, just as hot-air balloons became *Montgolfiers*.

On their December 1 flight, Charles and Robert ascended 2,000 feet and drifted twenty-seven miles to a gentle landing. Two friends, the Dukes de Chartres and de Fitz-James, galloped up to greet them, then Charles decided to go up once more alone. The Charlière ascended swiftly to 9,000 feet, where Charles felt an excruciating pain in his ears. He gazed about at the sunset, jettisoned some gas through his valve, and came down, never to go up again.

Old Ben Franklin drove home thinking about what Charlières could do in preventing warfare. He wrote to a friend, Dr. John Ingen-Hausz, "Convincing sovereigns of the folly of war may perhaps be one effect of it, since it will be impracticable for the most potent of them to guard his dominions. Five thousand balloons, capable of raising two men each, could cost no more than five ships of the line; and where is the prince who can afford so to cover his country with troops for its defense as that ten thousand men descending from the clouds might not in many places do an infinite deal of mischief, before a force could be brought together to repel them?" Thus the American statesman accurately predicted the use of airborne armies during World War II. Even in Franklin's time, insular England saw the danger, for with such aerial fleets the English Channel would no longer afford protection.

The honor of making the first balloon ascension from British soil went to an Italian, Vincent Lunardi, secretary to Prince Carmanico, the Neapolitan ambassador to England. Lunardi, a handsome fellow, planned to ascend from the enclosed gardens of a military hospital at Chelsea near London. To raise funds for his silken hydrogen balloon, Lunardi offered to split proceeds from exhibiting the apparatus with the invalided soldiers, but construction of the balloon had scarcely begun when competition appeared. A French balloonist, Monsieur Moret, showed up with a Montgolfier to beat Lunardi to the honors. A crowd of 60,000 spectators assembled on August 10, 1784, but, Lunardi reported disgustedly, "Every effort to inflate it seemed to fail, and the balloon sank into the fire which expanded it. The mob rushed in, tore it in a thousand pieces, robbed many of the company, leveled all the fences, and spread desolation and terror throughout the district."

Lunardi blamed the balloon riot on "the national prejudice of the English against the French" and came close to abandoning his own project, but suddenly changed his mind. "My perseverence," he wrote to his guardian, the Chevalier Compagni, "has given me an air of heroism which you know interests the fair sex. Many of the ladies wish they might accompany me, and with that bewitching air of sincerity which is almost peculiar to the women of this country, and which I think more difficult to resist than the coquetry of my own, they express a tender concern for my safety, which fixes my determinations: I will ascend, if I do it from the street!"

It didn't take the handsome Lunardi long to raise a bodyguard of 500 officers and men of the London Militia, headed by its Captain-General, the Prince of Wales himself. Thus fortified, Lunardi removed his balloon from Chelsea to the London Artillery House grounds and at 2:05 P.M. on September 24 "the last gun was fired, the cords divided, and the balloon rose."

Lunardi's historic voyage was a complete success. At a height of 200 yards he gazed down on a crowd of 150,-000 yelling and cheering fans and in return gaily waved a pair of flags, pumping away with two silken oars in an attempt to row across the sky. One oar broke, but Lunardi had the presence of mind to hail the Prince of Wales, just as a pigeon he'd taken aloft escaped from its cage. A dog and a cat were his other companions.

As he rose higher, Lunardi performed a ceremony that would become traditional to ballooning through the years—he uncorked a bottle of wine and toasted the world below. Next he found a leg of chicken, but threw

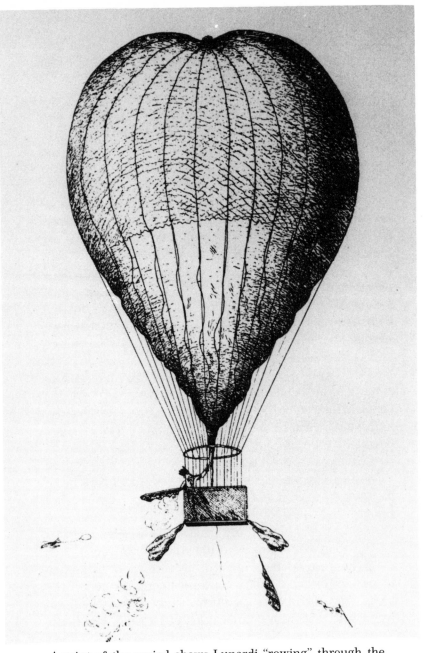

A print of the period shows Lunardi "rowing" through the sky with one oar after the other oar broke.

overboard the rest of his lunch, which had been covered with ballast sand.

Lunardi sailed on, gaily singing Italian arias at the top of his lungs and pumping away with his single oar, for more than half an hour. Fatigued, he finally put aside the oar and, he reported, "again had recourse to my bottle. This I emptied to the health of my friends and benefactors in the lower world."

Lunardi gazed about in awe at the neat hedgerows of England and marveled at meandering rivers, cities and towns and villages spread out below, the glistening sea in the distance. He jotted down his thoughts and posted a letter to Prince Carmanico by fastening it to his corkscrew and tossing it overboard, followed by the bottle, "which took some time disappearing."

Flushed with excitement and champagne, Lunardi worked his oar briskly again and found the balloon at last descending whether because or in spite of his efforts. He landed at 3:30 P.M. in a cornfield, where his cat and dog took off at a run and were never seen again. Friends arrived from London on horseback, and the whole party retired to a roadside tavern, the Bull Inn, where a celebration raged far into the night.

3

UP, UP,
AND AWAY!

The first American balloonist was Dr. John Jeffries, a Boston medical student who after the American Revolution went abroad to England to study medicine and there met an itinerant French aeronaut, Jean-Pierre Blanchard. Blanchard proposed crossing the English Channel in a balloon, and Dr. Jeffries agreed to finance the project, if he could go along.

The historic crossing took place January 7, 1785, starting from Dover Castle. Half way across, the balloon lost so much gas through leaks that it sank perilously close to the waves. Overboard went everything they could lay hands on—all ballast, silk oars, coats, hats, even Monsieur Blanchard's trousers. The balloon finally cleared the cliffs of France near Cape Blanez, then again settled over the Forest of Guines. Dr. Jeffries ended the voyage by grabbing a tree-top.

Jean-Pierre Blanchard's Channel balloon crossed from England to France on January 7, 1785, carrying the world's first air-mail letter.

Aboard the Channel balloon they carried the world's first air-mail letter, written in London by Franklin's royalist son, William Franklin, to the American statesman's grandson and secretary, William Temple Franklin. The balloonists were greeted in Paris at a warm reception attended by another noted American, Thomas Jefferson, who was in Europe to replace Franklin as Minister to France. Jefferson, like Franklin, saw danger in the military potential of ballooning and expressed his fears in a letter to Francis Hopkinson, one of the signers of the American Declaration of Independence:

"What think you of these balloons? This discovery seems to threaten the prostration of fortified works unless they can be closed from above, the destruction of fleets and what not. The French may now run over their laces, wines, etc. to England duty free. The whole system of British statutes made on the supposition of goods being brought into some port must be revised. Inland countries may become maritime states unless you choose rather to call them aerial ones as their commerce is in the future to be carried on through that element. But jesting apart I think that there is no longer a difficulty how Congress may move backwards and forwards, and your bungling scheme of moving houses and towns is now superceded. We shall soar sublime above the clouds."

It had been a private joke between Jefferson and Hopkinson, how to go about settling the young nation's capital in one place. Washington, D.C., the world's first planned national capital, would not come into existence until the next century. Congress already had met in eight cities—Philadelphia, Baltimore, Lancaster, York, Princeton, Annapolis, Trenton, and New York.

On March 12, Hopkinson replied from Philadelphia to

Jefferson's letter: "We have not taken the affair of the Balloons in hand. A high-flying politician is I think not unlike a balloon—he is full of inflammability, he is driven along by every current of wind—and those who will suffer themselves to be carried up by them run the risk that the bubble might burst and let them fall from the height to which the principle of levity had raised them."

Hopkinson's letter is of special historical interest, for it makes no mention of an alleged American ascension reported in the *Journal de Paris* under the dateline Philadelphia, Dec. 29, 1783. In that story, Hopkinson was named as sponsor of a flight, made by a carpenter, James Wilcox. Surely Hopkinson would have written Jefferson about it, so the story can be dismissed as a hoax.

On June 19, 1785, Jefferson wrote another letter to James Monroe, then attending Congress in New York, telling him of the tragic death of Pilatre de Rozier, the world's first aeronaut. Rozier had waited for months for a fair wind from France, to attempt the first Channel crossing by air to England. At 7 o'clock on the evening of June 15 a brisk wind sprang up from out of the southwest. Rozier and a companion, Monsieur P. A. Romain, immediately prepared for launch. Their aerial machine was a combination affair called a Charlo-Montgolfier—a hydrogen bag for primary lift, with a hot-air balloon suspended beneath, by which Rozier hoped to regulate his altitude without discharging ballast.

For two years each balloon type had been championed. Enthusiasm for both the Charlière and the Montgolfier ran high as the sport caught on. Marie Antoinette, Louis XVI's attractive wife, daringly appeared alone at masked balls in balloon dresses, and everywhere France's leading aeronauts were hailed as heroes, much as astronauts would be two centuries later.

Rozier hoped to combine the good points of both balloon types in his Channel balloon and so keep public enthusiasm alive; already the seeds of France's revolution had been planted; the gay days of court life were on the wane. Thus the flight began on a tense note, as Rozier shook hands with the Marquis de Maisonfort and shoved off for London.

The smoking aerostat rose more than a mile in the summer evening, drifting toward England, then was seen to swing back toward land, driven by a shifting wind. The craft billowed black smoke as Rozier tried vainly to rise above the errant wind. Suddenly the balloon glowed a bright orange and was engulfed in flames, as sparks ignited the hydrogen. The aeronauts plunged to their deaths before a horrified witness, Rozier's own fiance, an English girl named Susan Dyer. The tragedy dampened much of the enthusiasm for ballooning, but the sport could not be stopped. The challenge was too great.

For the next decade the balloon craze swept across most of Europe, until the French Revolution and the Napoleonic Wars changed the course of history. In 1794 balloons were used for the first time as military observation posts, realizing Franklin's prophesies.

Ballooning played an interesting role in the coronation of Emperor Napoleon in 1804. Napoleon organized an aeronautic corps under André-Jacques Garnerin, who made the world's first parachute jump from a balloon in 1797, and it was Garnerin who hit upon the idea of announcing Napoleon's coronation to the world by balloon.

On the night of December 11, 1804, nine days after the ceremony, the coronation balloon rose majestically

An elaborate balloon announced Napoleon's coronation.

from the square in front of Notre Dame, blazing with colored lights and with the news circling the circumference in gilt letters: *"Paris, 25 Frimaire, An XIII., Couronnement de L'Empereur Napoleon par S.S. Sie VII."*

The crowd cheered and the balloon was soon forgotten, until the next dawn when citizens of Rome saw a giant globe drifting over St. Peter's and the Vatican. It sank close to earth, snagged on a corner of Nero's tomb, then dropped into the waters of Lake Bracciano. This was too much for Napoleon—people snickered that Nero had done him in. Garnerin was dismissed and his place as aeronautic chief given to the wife of Jean-Pierre Blanchard, herself an able balloonist.

On March 20, 1811, Madame Blanchard announced the birth of the new King of Rome by scattering bulletins from her balloon. She supervised many other public fetes, the last one at Tivoli on July 6, 1819, when she outdid Garnerin's coronation balloon by carrying aloft a supply of Bengal lights and skyrockets.

An eyewitness reported: "The balloon rose splendidly, to the sound of music and the shoutings of the people. A rain of gold and thousands of stars fell from the car as it ascended. A moment of calm, and then an unexpected light appeared. . . . The light increased, then disappeared suddenly; then appeared again, in the form of an immense jet of blazing gas. The terrible glare was perceived from the boulevards and all the Quartier Montmartre. The spectators cried 'Brava! Vive Madame Blanchard!' thinking she was giving them an unexpected treat." The burning balloon was seen to descend and strike a rooftop in the Rue de Provence, spilling Madame Blanchard to the street below, where she died of a broken neck.

Madame Blanchard was not, however, the world's

Madame Thible was the first woman to go aloft in a balloon on June 4, 1784.

first female aeronaut. It was another Frenchwoman, Madame Thible, a popular operatic singer, who ascended from Lyon on June 4, 1784, in a Montgolfier balloon, *La Gustave*, with Monsieur Fleurant, a painter, singing lustily "Oh, To Travel in the Clouds!"

The first female balloonist in England was a rather portly woman who afterward published an account of her adventure in a pamphlet titled "A Letter Addressed To a Female Friend. By Mrs. Letitia Sage, the First English Female Aerial Traveller." Mrs. Sage appeared at St. George's Fields, Newington Butts, an amusement garden near London, on June 29, 1785, a fortnight after the death of Pilatre de Rozier. A crowd of 100,000 morbid spectators watched as she stepped into the car of Vincent Lunardi's balloon, with Lunardi and George Biggin, a wealthy patron of the arts. The flight, which lasted an hour, was a huge success. Lunardi landed in a field near Harrow School, where Mrs. Sage stepped out, relieving the balloon, she wrote, of "two hundred pounds of human weight." An irate farmer threatened to destroy the balloon in repayment for damage to his crops caused by the landing, but, Mrs. Sage reported, "the heroic boys of Harrow School saved the balloon from destruction."

The earliest aerostatic experiment carried out in England was the work of Count Francesco Zambeccari, an Italian sailor of fortune who fled to London to escape the Spanish Inquisition for some unrecorded misdeed. On November 4, 1783, Zambeccari released a five-foot hot-air balloon from a rooftop in Cheapside and three weeks later sent up another twice the size.

By December, 1784, Zambeccari was ready to ascend himself, in a hydrogen balloon thirty-four feet in diameter, which supported a gaily decorated boat. He took along a passenger, Admiral Sir Edward Vernon, but had to eject from the boat, "with gentle force," an attractive Miss Grist. She was, he explained, only an "accidental passenger" who had climbed aboard for a thrill.

High above the clouds Zambeccari discovered the valve rope had been inadvertently sealed inside the balloon, when he patched a hole prior to launch. To come down, he drew a knife and slit the balloon silk. They landed thirty-three miles from London safe and sound. A second attempt to ascend from England ended in a riot, when things went wrong and spectators stormed the launch platform to get their money back.

Zambeccari left England in disgust and took up a more adventurous life. He went to Russia, became a lieutenant in the Czar's navy, was shipwrecked in the Dardanelles, captured by the Turks, jailed for two years, then returned to ballooning at Bologna in 1812. On September 12 that year, he met the same fate as Rozier— his combination hot-air hydrogen balloon caught fire. He hurled himself over the side, rather than burn to death.

In later years another adventurous soul, the German pioneer glider enthusiast Otto Lilienthal, wrote that he was inspired to take up aeronautics after reading, *The Travels of Count Zambeccari*. In this autobiography Zambeccari described an epic adventure over the Adriatic on October 7, 1804, with two companions named Andreoli and Grassetti, when he attempted to steer 'the balloon with a jet of flame from an ingenious lamp filled with "spirits of wine" (alcohol). On a trial flight, the Count accidentally set himself afire; the heat from his burning clothing sent the balloon careening skyward before he could extinguish the flames.

Sailing along over Bologna, with his two friends, Zambeccari recalled: "The lamp became useless. I had

Zambeccari and his friends
were rescued by boat,
hours after their balloon
had fallen into the Adriatic.

neglected to take nourishment for twenty-four hours, and with my weariness I fell to the floor of the balloon gallery in a profound sleep, like death." High in the cold night sky, he suddenly awoke and cried: "Where are we? What time is it?"

It was 2 o'clock in the morning, the compass was broken, the lantern wouldn't light, and no one knew where they were—just somewhere in the thin air above a cloud layer. Suddenly the silence was broken by sound of distant breakers.

"I immediately seized a large sack of sand," he related, "but had no time to throw it over before we were all in the water, gallery and all. In the first moment of fright,

we threw into the sea everything that would lighten the balloon—our ballast, all our instruments, a portion of our own clothing, our money, and the oars. As the balloon still did not rise we threw over the lamp also.

"The balloon suddenly rose all at once, with such rapidity and to such a prodigious elevation that we had difficulty in hearing each other, even shouting at the top of our voices. I was ill, and vomited severely. Grassetti was bleeding at the nose; we were both breathing short and hard. The cold seized us and we found ourselves coated with ice. The moon, in its last quarter, looked red as blood.

"About 4 in the morning we fell again into the sea,

somewhere in the middle of the Adriatic. At daybreak we found ourselves opposite Pesaro, four miles from shore. Several boats came by, but no sooner did they see the balloon than they made all sail to get away from it. Finally one small one sent a longboat to us."

Zambeccari's troubles were not yet over; when the sailors attached a rope to the balloon and helped the aeronauts aboard the longboat, the balloon shot skyward, spilling everybody out of the boat. The rope was cut and away the balloon soared, to disappear from sight in the clouds. Zambeccari suffered frostbite on his harrowing misadventure in the clouds, and had to have his fingers amputated. His tale was worthy of any adventure produced by Jules Verne, himself a balloon enthusiast discussed in a later chapter.

4

BALLOONING
IN THE
NEW WORLD

Balloon activity in America was quick to follow its appearance in European skies, and among the first to grasp its potential was Gen. George Washington. After resigning his army commission and settling down at Mount Vernon, Washington's imagination was stirred by the possible use of balloons to open up the interior of the new nation.

On April 4, 1784, he wrote to a friend in Paris, Maj. Gen. Duportail: "I have only newspaper accounts of air-balloons, to which I do not know what credence to give; as the tales related of them are marvelous, and lead us to suspect, that our own friends at Paris in a little time will come flying through the air, instead of ploughing the ocean to get to America. . . ."

In Philadelphia Dr. John Foulke, physician to the Pennsylvania Hospital, was at this time busily at work on a six-foot diameter Montgolfier, a copy of early French balloons he watched ascend over Paris during a visit there. Francis Hopkinson wrote to Jefferson about it and exclaimed: "The name of Congress is almost forgotten, and for every person that will mention that respectable body, a hundred will talk of an air balloon!"

On May 12 Hopkinson again wrote Jefferson, with news of the first balloon ascent from American soil: "We have been amusing ourselves with raising air balloons made of paper," he penned. "The first that mounted our atmosphere was made by Dr. Foulke and sent up from the garden of the Minister of Holland the day before yesterday. Yesterday forenoon the same balloon was raised from Mr. Morris's garden, and last evening another was exhibited at the Minister of France's to the great amusement of the spectators. They rose twice or perhaps three times the height of the houses, and then gently descended without damage."

To Hopkinson, like Franklin, a balloon was little more than a newly born babe with an uncertain future. On May 24 he wrote Franklin: "This discovery, like electricity, magnetism, and many other important phenomena, serves for amusement at first—its uses and applications will hereinafter unfold themselves. There may be many mechanical means of giving a balloon progressive motion, other than what the current of wind would give it."

Hopkinson went on to suggest a streamlined balloon shaped like a wherry fish, with a paddlewheel at the stern, adding: "there is no doubt but that it would (in a calm at least) give the machine progressive motion, upon the same principle that a boat is sculled through the water."

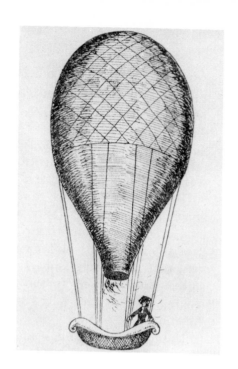

A contemporary print shows the balloon launched at a fiesta in Puebla, Mexico, on July 11, 1785.

Overlooked by historians was a flurry of balloon activity in Mexico, where reports of the Montgolfiers' success in France spurred hot-air experimentation early in 1784. On May 19, the *Gazeta de Mexico* published the first notice of an intended ascent, but there is no record that it took place. However, the following February a regimental captain at Tlaxcala, Don Antonio Maria Fernandez, reportedly sent up a 6½-foot paper balloon, and on July 11, 1785, at a fiesta in Puebla, a gaily decorated balloon was launched with a dummy passenger "to represent the valorous European aeronauts."

Of all early accounts of ballooning in America, most intriguing was a story that appeared in the *Maryland Journal and Baltimore Advertiser* early in 1784, about the efforts of a young Baltimore attorney, Peter Carnes, to navigate the air. On June 19 that year Carnes attempted a tethered ascent from Bladensburg, Maryland, but the balloon was damaged when it struck a tree. On June 25, the same paper related that Carnes drew a sizable crowd to Baltimore, where his thirty-six-foot diameter hot-air machine tugged at its ropes. The reporter wrote: "Ambition, on this occasion, so fired the youthful heart of a lad (only thirteen years old!) of the name of Edward Warren, that he bravely embarked as a volunteer, and behaved with the steady fortitude of an old voyager." Young Edward thus became the first to ascend in America.

The following month, on July 17, 25,000 curious people gathered in Philadelphia's Centre Square to watch the hanging of two street robbers, John Downie and John Martin, then moved on to the Walnut Street Prison for a better show—Peter Carnes was going to outdo what young Edward Warren had done, with a free ascent. Despite an advancing storm, he stepped into the basket beneath the bulging globe of silk and signaled to the ground crew: "Hands off!"

Just as the balloon was released, a gust of wind slammed the basket against the prison wall; Carnes tumbled to the ground. Outside, the assembled thousands cheered lustily, believing Carnes to be still aboard as it swept off into the squalling sky. "Small as a whiskey keg," the balloon was seen suddenly to glow like a blazing meteor and plunge to earth. Not until the following day did the crowd learn Carnes had escaped a terrible fate—and lost the honor of becoming America's first free balloonist.

Philip Freneau, a contemporary American poet, was moved to write prophetically in *Freeman's Journal* that year:

> The stagemen, whose gallopers scarce have the power
> Through the dirt to convey you ten miles an hour,
> When advanced to balloon shall so furiously drive
> You'll hardly know whether you're dead or alive.
> The man who at Boston sets out with the sun,
> If the wind should be fair, may be with us at one;
> At Gunpowder Ferry drink whiskey at three,
> And at six be at Edentown, ready for tea.
> At Charleston by ten he for sleep shall prepare,
> And by twelve the next day be the devil knows where.
> If Britain should ever disturb us again,
> (As they threaten to do in the next George's reign),
> No doubt they will play us a set of new tunes,
> And pepper us well with their fighting balloons.

The race to become the first free aeronaut in America was on, yet a decade elapsed after the birth of ballooning in France in 1783, before a successful free ascent took place this side of the Atlantic. During those years Yankee experimentation progressed slowly, with both hot-air and hydrogen bags. In the spring of 1786 the Rev. James Madison, of the College of William and Mary in Williamsburg, Virginia, wrote Jefferson about his concern over the lack of scientific study.

"We raise here small balloons filled with inflammable air," he reported. "I have once made a trial of pit coal; we raise those filled with rarefied air, tolerably large (about twenty feet diam.), but I believe no one in America has yet ventured to mount with a balloon." To Madison, balloons offered a means of investigating the lapse rate of temperature and density of the atmosphere at different elevations, of studying the propagation of sounds, and the descent of bodies.

On September 23, 1789 Joseph Deeker, an Englishman, attempted an ascent from New York City, as part of a celebration honoring George Washington's inauguration as first constitutional President of the United States. Congress, then in session in New York, adjourned "to see the balloon let off." Unfortunately, Deeker's balloon burst into flames and the show was cancelled.

Jean-Pierre Blanchard, the French balloonist, was a veteran of more than forty European ascensions when he visited America in 1792, and advertised that he would ascend from the Walnut Street Prison court in Philadelphia the following January 9. It was the same launch site

used by Peter Carnes, but Blanchard had a better balloon, inflated with hydrogen.

George Washington was there early, greeted by a fifteen-gun salute by a company of artillery, and he cheered with the others as Blanchard rose skyward, waving the colors of the United States and the new French Republic. He carried a "passport" signed by Washington, appealing to citizens not to molest him. It was a good thing, for when he landed in a field across the river in New Jersey a group of farmers, carrying long rifles, approached menacingly. The passport saved the day.

Successful though the flight was, Blanchard lost money on it—his expenses ran to $2,500 while his gate receipts, at $5 each, totaled only $405. On subsequent ascents the results were the same; New World citizens

When Jean-Pierre Blanchard landed his balloon in a New Jersey field in 1792 he was met by frightened farmers, two of them carrying rifles.

had other uses for their money. He finally tried to arouse interest by announcing he would go up in a "wonderful carriage propelled by an automaton in the shape of an eagle, chained to the tongue of the carriage and guided by the traveler."

Even the idea of an eagle-powered airship failed to draw customers. Blanchard, in disgust, returned to Europe, where he recouped his losses with ascents from Paris, Rouen, Lyons, and elsewhere. His sixtieth and last ascent was from The Hague in February, 1808. Siezed with an apoplectic fit in midair, Blanchard tumbled to the ground, fatally injured. He died the following year.

For a number of years visiting European aeronauts made ascents in America, with little better financial luck than Blanchard's. In the fall of 1819 two Frenchmen, Messieurs Michel and Stanislaus, announced an ascent from Philadelphia's Vauxhall Gardens, planning to go up 2,000 feet and parachute back to earth. A crowd of 30,-000 skeptical people showed up, and by dusk the balloon was barely one-quarter full. The crowd grew ugly, toppled the fence surrounding the balloon, ripped the balloon to shreds, smashed the acid barrels, then proceeded to burn down the main building. By 9 o'clock Vauxhall Gardens was a smouldering ruin. Commented the *United States Gazette*: "A mobbing spirit has not been characteristic of Philadelphia, and it is with regret that we publish that such a disgraceful riot has taken place."

Eugene Robertson, a countryman of Blanchard's, was more cautious when he staged the first balloon ascension from New York City on July 9, 1825—he refused to go up until a subscription of $1,200 had been raised. The ascent finally took place from Castle Garden, at the tip of Manhattan, where a special tent was provided for the guest of honor, Marie Joseph Paul Yves Roch Gilbert Du Motier, the sixty-seven-year-old Marquis de Lafayette. The old soldier, who had helped Washington win the Revolution, was making his first visit to America in half a century, and a special celebration was held in his honor at New York's Battery Park.

Robertson's balloon, twenty-one feet in diameter, was filled with 5,875 cubic feet of hydrogen, generated on the spot by a new method of water decomposition. Seats were only twenty-five cents each, but for $15 Robertson offered to take up passengers for a short captive ascent. There were no takers. At 7 o'clock the elderly Marquis cut the rope and Robertson shot skyward, waving flags at the crowd.

The Castle Garden ascent was Robertson's fifth, and his first in America. His father, Professor Etienne Gaspard

A crowd gathered at the tip of Manhattan Island to watch Eugene Robertson's balloon ascent from Castle Garden.

Etienne Gaspard Robertson's design for an airship, the *Sacrum Minerva*, large enough to carry sixty men.

Robertson, had made more than fifty ascents in Europe, and had delighted the world with a fanciful plan to build a seventy-ton airship, the *Sacrum Minerva*, large enough to carry sixty men on a transatlantic voyage to last several months. Robertson's brother, Dimitri, made the first ascent from India at Calcutta in 1835.

America's first female aeronaut was a young woman named Madame Johnson, who announced she would go up in Robertson's balloon from Castle Garden on October 18, 1825. High winds forced a postponement until the 20th. The New York *Evening Post* reported: "The balloon being well inflated, the gondola was attached and the lady Aeronaut made her appearance. She is about thirty-five years of age, and was dressed in a white satin gown, with a red spencer. She gave the word to let go, bade her friends farewell, waved her flags, and rose with great rapidity, amidst the shouts of the surrounding multitude." Madame Johnson sailed across the East River and Brooklyn and landed in a marsh "without the least injury except getting wet."

Robertson made a few more ascents from Castle Garden, one with a woman identified only as "Mlle. M'C****" with whom he shared a glass of champagne high above the city. Robertson next went up alone, reaching a height of 21,000 feet, an American altitude record that would stand for some time. After further ascensions from New Orleans in 1827, Robertson introduced ballooning to Havana, Cuba, early in 1828. His last ascent was from Vera Cruz, Mexico, where he died in 1836 of yellow fever.

On a brief trip to Europe in 1828, Robertson had taken along a brilliant American youth, twenty-one-year-old Charles Ferson Durant, who saw in ballooning a means of exploring the upper atmosphere, studying storm clouds in formation, and seeking to discover the origin of the "electric fluid" that mysteriously leaped to earth as lightning. In 1830 Durant would return to the United States well trained by Robertson, as the first American-born aeronaut.

5

THE
BALLOONATICS

In four short years from 1830 to 1834, Charles Ferson Durant, the first American balloonist, accomplished one dozen successful ascents and fired the imagination of a new generation of adventurous men and women, whose achievements in the sky would rival those of veteran European aeronauts. On his first of six ascensions from New York's Castle Garden, on September 10, 1830, he was an unknown, identified by the New York *Evening Post* only as "a person named Durant."

The paper added, "We understand the aeronaut came safely to land on the farm of Mr. Johnson, near South Amboy." A subsequent edition reported that "about 6 o'clock the balloon was discovered gliding gently but rapidly over Perth Amboy, at an elevation judged at a mile and a half. By the aid of a sky glass, the aerial voyager was distinctly seen waving his flag."

Durant quickly became a hero. He was carried on the shoulders of the Jerseyites through the streets and placed aboard a steamer, the *Thistle*, to return to New York, but not before he was approached by a wide-eyed youth clutching a strange-looking model airship which the boy claimed would sail *into the wind*. The youth, Solomon Andrews, begged Durant to take his model into the sky and drop it, but Durant, flushed with success, declined.

Andrews, like Durant, was a youth with remarkable mechanical ingenuity. He was first inspired to fly when he gazed out the window of his father's church while listening to the elder Andrews deliver a lengthy sermon to a dozing congregation, and spotted an eagle soaring. He wrote later: "I caught as with an electric shock the key to the whole system of flight. From that moment my aim of life was fixed."

One by one, Andrews approached other balloonists to take his machine into the upper atmosphere and drop it, and when none would help him, he decided to go ahead and build a man-sized airship on his own. In 1849, the year of the big California gold rush, curious citizens of Perth Amboy watched him erect a huge shed in a vacant field. On the Fourth of July that year, they would find out what he'd been building inside America's first airship hangar. Andrews had not been idle since the day he met Charles Durant nineteen years earlier. Through those years he worked hard as a public servant and inventor and held onto his secret dream—to fly. Rising from a simple Justice of the Peace to a three-term Mayor of Perth Amboy, he also found time to invent and patent more than a score of ideas, the most profitable being a combination lock which led to a government contract to make foolproof padlocks for mail sacks.

It had been Andrews's notion not to reveal his airship

until he was ready to sail off to New York, but the appearance of a rival inventor, Rufus Porter, changed his mind. Porter had formed a stock company to promote an airship line to California's gold-rush country, and Andrews decided it was high time to unveil his invention. On June 21 he filed a caveat with the U. S. Patent Office and inserted an ad in the New York *Sun*. Andrews let the public know he planned to show off his airship on July 4, but added mysteriously, "Whoever shall discover the motive power and its mode of action shall be entitled to a share of stock in the invention."

What the public saw was impressive enough—a huge framework eighty feet long, twenty feet wide, and ten feet deep, suspended from the ceiling. *Knickerbocker Magazine* in New York reported that "thousands of dollars have been expended in the project, and the proprietor has obtained permission to cross the Atlantic and descend through the roof of the great glass palace in Hyde Park, London."

Having established his priority, Andrews closed the hangar doors and didn't open them again for several more years. At the outbreak of the Civil War he joined the Union Army and served on the Sanitary Commission, caring for wounded soldiers on transports, until he met

An engraving of Rufus Porter's *Aeroport*

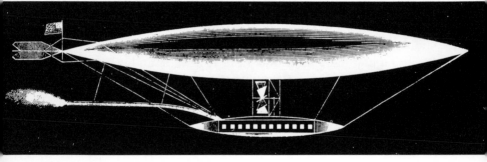

Professor Thaddeus Lowe, the celebrated Yankee aeronaut who headed up Lincoln's Balloon Corps.

Andrews sat down and wrote a letter to Lincoln, requesting government funds to finish his airship, and offering as collateral real estate holdings he valued at $50,000. "I will sail the airship five to ten miles into Secessia and back again, or no pay," he added. When his efforts were pigeonholed, Andrews again went ahead on his own.

He bought 1,200 yards of Irish linen and made three cylindrical gas bags, each eighty feet long and thirteen feet in diameter. Into these he stuffed twenty-one smaller balloonets. The cylindrical bags were laced together like cigars, and beneath them he slung a catwalk twelve feet long. In June, 1863, Andrews, then fifty-seven, at last made his maiden flight in his strange airship, which he called the *Aereon*, meaning "air age." The flight was moderately successful, but the interior ballonets collapsed from leakage. Andrews substitued cloth partitions to keep the gas evenly distributed.

Amazingly enough, the *Aereon* worked. Andrews's secret was simple—it was based on gravity power. When the *Aereon* ascended at a tilted angle, it shot forward like a plank rising in water, at a speed estimated at better than 30 mph, directly into the wind. It even boasted an angle-of-attack indicator, with three marbles in calibrated wooden grooves. The New York *Herald* reported one flight on September 4, 1863:

"Andrews set her off in a spiral course upwards, she going at a high rate of speed and describing circles in the air of more than one and a half miles in circumference. She made twenty revolutions before she entered the first strata of dense white clouds, about two miles high, scattering them in all directions."

Following the flight (made without Andrews aboard, but with 130 pounds of ballast at the rear of the cat-walk), the inventor destroyed his *Aereon* to prevent her secret from becoming known to the Rebs. The war ended without its assistance, but Andrews won a patent in 1864 and the next year formed the Aerial Navigation Company, America's first chartered airline with an actual airship.

He next built a lemon-shaped *Aereon*, from four war surplus balloons left over from Professor Lowe's operations, and on May 25, 1866, took her up over New York City with three passengers aboard, Dr. G. Waldo Hill, Charles M. Plumb, and George B. Trow, all officers of the Aerial Navigation Company.

On this flight, and a subsequent one with only Charles Plumb aboard, Andrews proved his *Aereon* really could navigate against the wind, by crossing and recrossing a designated landmark a number of times. Although the thing worked, a bank failure plunged the Aerial Navigation Company heavily into debt and the project was abandoned, but not before Solomon Andrews realized his lifelong dream, of flying on gravity power.

One hundred years later a group of New Jersey investigators renewed Solomon Andrews's concept with a brand new *Aereon*. They built a full-sized ship that actually flew with a small motor attached but were unble to raise enough capital to build a larger cargo-hauler. The project was put aside.

Motive power was, from the beginning, the main challenge to dirigible makers. It was not enough simply to escape from earth. The big problem, recognized by observers from Benjamin Franklin and George Washington on down, was to give lighter-than-air craft forward mobility.

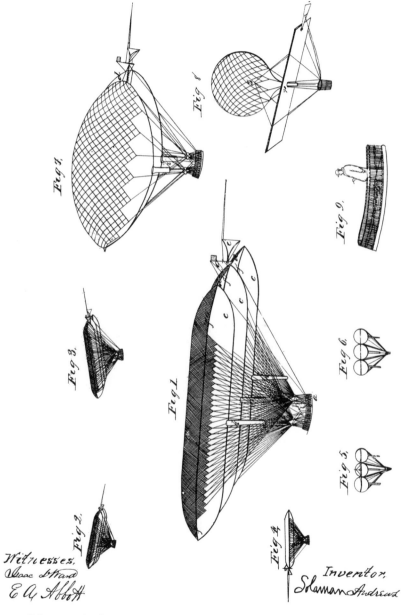

Solomon Andrews was given a patent in 1864 based on
these designs for airships.

Among the more fanciful schemes was one proposed by a Frenchman, Edmond Charles Genet, at about the time balloonist Robertson was thrilling crowds at New York's Castle Garden. Genet obtained a U. S. Patent on his contraption, a horse-powered dirigible, on October 31, 1825, and published a pamphlet describing how it worked. The idea was immediately challenged by Dr. Thomas P. Jones, editor of the eminent *Franklin Journal and Mechanics Magazine.* Jones ridiculed it as "a monstrous balloon, which is to be loaded with a windmill and two horses, their attendants, a chemical apparatus, an anchor, fodder and provender, water, provisions for three men, and errors and omissions to the amount of 13,400 pounds."

A detailed plan of Edmond Charles Genet's two-horsepower dirigible

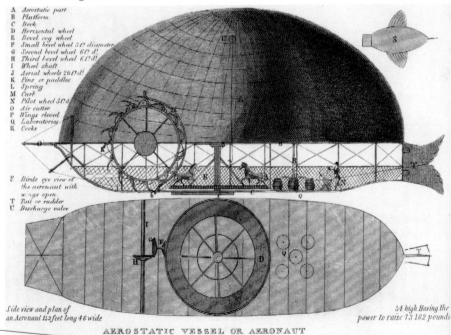

A   *Aerostatic part*
B   *Platform*
C   *Deck*
D   *Horizontal wheel*
E   *Bevel cog wheel*
F   *Small bevel wheel 3 f.t diameter*
G   *Second bevel wheel 6 ft. d.*
H   *Third bevel wheel 6 ft. d.*
I   *Wheel shaft*
J   *Aerial wheels 26 ft d.*
K   *Fins or paddles*
L   *Spring*
M   *Carl*
N   *Pilot wheel 5 ft. d.*
O   *Air cutter*
P   *Wings closed*
Q   *Laboratories*
R   *Cocks*

S   *Birds eye view of the aeronaut with wings open*
T   *Tail or rudder*
U   *Discharge valve*

Side view and plan of an Aeronaut 152 feet long 46 wide

54 high Having the power to raise 73.162 pounds

AEROSTATIC VESSEL OR AERONAUT

Genet patiently tried to explain his idea. There were "two different kinds of upward forces in fluids, the one due to the principle of gravity, the other to what I call the principle of levity." Here he got in over his head, claiming that levity was "due to the action of another fluid, which draws upward toward the etherial regions, certain particles of matter and aerial fluids, in proportion to their degree of affinity with the unknown cause of that ascensive and centrifugal force."

What Genet was trying to say was that there was something strange going on, something similar to the then popular theory that the sun drew up moisture from the oceans along its slanting rays. Another contemporary was kinder to Genet. Benjamin Silliman, editor of the *American Journal of Science and Arts*, wrote: "There is a wide difference between attempting that which is absurd, and that which is only very difficult. Perpetual motion is an absurdity, but it involves no absurdity to attempt to rise into the atmosphere, or to steer our way when we have arrived there."

In 1793 Genet was appointed French Minister to the United States, but was recalled when he began organizing military expeditions against Florida and Louisiana and commissioning privateers to prey on British shipping. He finally settled in America, married the daughter of the postmaster general, Samuel Osgood, and turned his attention to ballooning. He tried in vain to interest Congress in financing construction of a "horse balloon" to search for a Northwest Passage through Arctic ice fields.

Other inventors were stimulated to try their hand at inventing navigable balloons by romantic reports of sky sailing by balloonist Charles Durant. After one Castle Garden ascension, Durant related how he had penetrated a cloud layer into the clear sky above: "Here burst upon my sight one of the most imposing views I have ever beheld. Call it majestic, splendid, or sublime—invoke a Shakespeare's mind to describe, or a painter's to portray it—they, and even thought must fail to conceive the rich downy softness and white fleecy accumulation of clouds piled in waves as far as the eye could reach, covering the earth, and closing to my sight the land, water, and everything that I had so long viewed with delight. Above me nothing but a clear and cerulean expanse—the golden sunbeams spreading over the vast ocean of clouds, extending through the immensity of space."

Most people in the early nineteenth century accepted ballooning as an adventurous sport, but to the Assiniboin Indians of the Northwest Territory it was bad medicine. In the winter of 1832 Maj. John F. A. Sanford, U. S. Indian Agent, had selected a tribesman, Wi-Jun-Jon, to represent his people on a good-will junket to Washington. Wi-Jun-Jon dutifully made the long-boat trip down the Missouri to St. Louis, notching a stick for each white man's house he saw. When he filled the stick with notches, he began notching the boat. At St. Louis, George Catlin, the noted American ethnologist, painted Wi-Jun-Jon's portrait, which appears today in Catlin's two-volume *Manners, Customs and Condition of the North American Indians*, in which his story is told.

In Washington Wi-Jun-Jon met the Great White Chief, Andrew Jackson, examined the warships, then traveled up to New York City by steamboat. There he watched Charles Durant make his sixth and last balloon ascension, from Castle Garden. Back home in Assiniboin country, Wi-Jun-Jon celebrated his return with a two-day drunk. Then, according to Catlin, he related what he had seen, the numbers of white people, the beauty of their squaws with their red cheeks, and the man who

No. 826,038.

PATENTED JULY 17, 1906.

J. KREMENOK.
AIR SHIP.
APPLICATION FILED DEO. 17, 1904.

2 SHEETS—SHEET 1

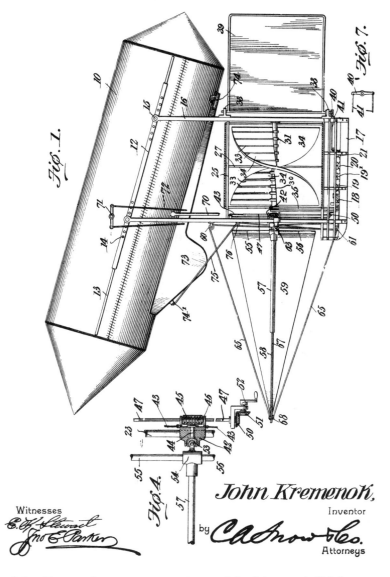

Witnesses

John Kremenok,
Inventor

by CA Snow & Co.
Attorneys

John Kremenok won a patent in 1906 for his metal dirigible but could not get financial backing to build it.

ascended to the Happy Hunting Ground in a big ball of gas.

Unquestionably, the other Assiniboins decided, Wi-Jun-Jon had gotten hold of some bad medicine that affected his mind. A young Indian solved the matter—he filed the handle of an iron stew-pot to a fine point, rammed it into the muzzle of his gun, and while Wi-Jun-Jon sat one evening at the campfire, spinning fantastic tales about a man who could fly, the stew-pot handle pierced the back of his head. Wi-Jun-Jon, whose Indian name meant "pigeon's egg head," died a martyr to the progress of aeronautics in America.

Aerial oddities continued to appear over the years, well into the twentieth century. On December 17, 1904 —just one year after the first successful flights of the Wright brothers at Kitty Hawk in a heavier-than-air craft —John Kremenok, a young Czech inventor living in Racine, Wisconsin, applied for a patent on an unusual metal dirigible driven by a huge archimedean screw propeller. Kremenok's daughter, Mrs. Arthur Brumm, recalled that he would lock himself in his study for days at a time, working on his invention, but after he won his patent he could find no backers. "He became despondent and morose and his health was gone," she remembered, "due to the strain of sleepless nights spent in his little room. After six years of discouragement he died in 1912, at the age of twenty-nine."

At the time Kremenok was working up plans for his metal airship, Peter Nissen, a circus acrobat, attempted to roll across Lake Michigan inside a balloon filled with air. The balloon reached the far shore, and when it was torn open by a curious crowd, Nissen was found frozen to death. His craft was promptly called the *Fool Killer*.

6

TO THE
POLES!

Ever since Benjamin Franklin first proposed ways to give balloons progressive motion in 1783, aeronauts envisioned using them to explore the world's unknown regions, from the mysterious frozen poles to the unreachable jungles of Africa. The first dirigible proposal of record to give balloons mobility was that of Capt. Jean Baptiste Marie Meusnier, of the French Army Corps of Engineers, who in 1783 presented his concept to the Academy of Sciences in Paris. The Meusnier craft was to be a magnificent ellipsoidal aerostat 261 feet long, designed to carry thirty men with provisions for sixty days. It was never built.

The following summer brothers Anne-Jean and M. N. Robert, who built Monsieur Charles's balloon, constructed a cylindrical vessel to be propelled by five parasol-shaped

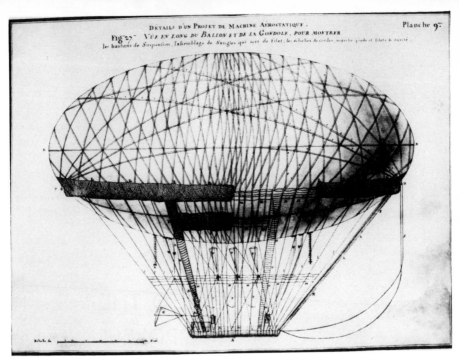

DÉTAILS D'UN PROJET DE MACHINE AÉROSTATIQUE.   Planche 9.

Fig. 27.   VUE EN LONG DU BALLON ET DE LA GONDOLE, POUR MONTRER
les haubans de Suspention, l'assemblage de Sangles qui sert de Filet, les échelles de cordes, marche-pieds et Filets de Sureté.

Jean Baptiste Marie Meusnier presented this plan for a dirigible to the French Academy of Science in 1783.

oars of blue taffeta, designed to open and close like a fish's gills. It didn't work. In 1785 more than one hundred entries were submitted to the Academy of Lyon, in a contest for the best dirigible design, but all were rejected as impractical.

Across the seas, a forgotten Baltimore inventor named John Pennington proposed the first dirigible in America in 1842, four years after he unsuccessfully sought a Congressional appropriation of $2,000 to build a kite-like steam-powered flying machine. Balloonist John Wise convinced Pennington to use a gas bag in place of the kite, and the result was a design for a 234-foot dirigible shaped like a pumpkin seed, powered with a steam engine using alcohol for fuel.

Pennington's Steam Balloon, as he called it, would have definite military use, he informed Congress, this time requesting a $10,000 appropriation. Washington turned a cold shoulder; the nation was still recovering from the financial panic of 1837. His proposal was referred to the Senate Committee on Military Affairs on March 29, 1842, and on July 8 to the Committee on Patents, where it was forgotten.

Five years later New York crowds were marveling at a six-foot long dirigible that flew in lazy circles around the auditorium of the Merchant's Exchange Building, driven by a spring-loaded propeller. The device was a

In 1842 John Pennington designed a 234-foot, steam-powered dirigible.

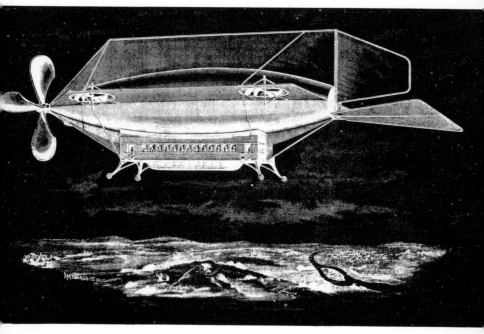

working model of a proposed 700-foot steam dirigible, the *Aeroport*, to carry 150 passengers at 90 mph from New York to the California gold fields. Its inventor was Rufus Porter, a Massachusetts Yankee who had also patented a cord-making machine, steam carriage, portable horse-powered saw, clock, cornhusker, churn, washing machine, signal telegraph, fire alarm, and horse-powered flatboat. His son, F. Rufus Porter, recalled that his father regretted inventing the horse-boat: "He felt it was cruelty to make a horse walk up hill all day on a treadmill, and was sorry he ever thought of the idea." Porter also invented the six-shooter and sold it to Samuel Colt for one hundred dollars, his son claimed.

He moved to New York City where in August, 1845, he founded the magazine *Scientific American*, which still exists today. Six months later he sold that journal and started a new one, the *Scientific Mechanic*, in which he published sketches of his proposed dirigible.

In Washington, D.C., Porter sought Congressional help, as had Pennington, but on a more ambitious scale. He built a twenty-foot model and installed a steam engine that drove two propellers. Below the gas bag hung a seven-foot car, with a row of tiny windows from which little dolls smiled at school children. Schools were let out to allow them to "witness the phenomenon of a steam vessel sailing through the air."

In 1852, unable to raise government backing, Porter formed the *Aerial Navigation Company* and announced plans to establish a transcontinental airline. Sales of stock brought in $3,895, with which he built a five-passenger *Aeroport*, 160 feet long, that carried a passenger salon sixty feet in length. Unusual features of the *Aeroport* included a method of attaching it to a mooring mast, parachutes for the passengers, and an airborne generating plant to replenish the gas. The craft was actually completed, but was wrecked in a sudden gale before Porter had a chance to fly it. With the onset of the Civil War the scheme was forgotten.

Other oddities appeared in the history of dirigible development, just as they had in ballooning. Among the more successful was an invention of Charles F. Ritchel, of Corry, Pennsylvania, who in 1878 won a patent for the first American flying machine to carry a man through the air and return him safely to the starting point.

Ritchel's machine was a twenty-five-foot cylindrical gas bag supporting a framework which the operator rode like a bicycle, steering it by changing the thrust line of a hand-cranked propeller with his feet. The crank also could rotate a propeller underneath the machine, to raise or lower it.

Ritchel was approached at Hartford by Buffalo Bill Cody's advance man, Sam Alexander, who arranged a series of demonstration flights by a ninety-six-pound youth named Quinlan. Billie Garvie, a Hartford reporter, remembers watching Quinlan perform when he was a lad of twelve: "The crowd was tense with excitement, and boys turned cartwheels in their ecstacy," he recalled. Quinlan sailed the machine out over the Connecticut River and back, turning it around in midair, rising and descending at will.

In 1880 Ritchel opened offices in New York City to solicit backing for a projected flight to the North Pole, which he estimated he could reach in ten days. "If the balloon be destroyed or exhausted, I am a lost man," he admitted, "but the risk is less than to any other arctic voyager!"

HARPER'S WEEKLY.

JOURNAL OF CIVILIZATION.

Vol. XXII.—No. 1124.]　　　NEW YORK, SATURDAY, JULY 13, 1878.　　　[WITH A SUPPLEMENT. PRICE TEN CENTS.

Entered according to Act of Congress, in the Year 1878, by Harper & Brothers, in the Office of the Librarian of Congress, at Washington.

The July 13, 1878, issue of *Harper's Weekly* featured a cover picture of Charles Ritchel aloft in his flying machine.

One serious attempt to reach the North Pole by air ended tragically for a Swedish aeronaut, Salomon August Andree, who was inspired to take up ballooning when he visited the Philadelphia World Exposition in 1876 and met the American aeronaut John Wise. On July 11, 1897, Andree sailed away from rugged Spitsbergen, Norway, in a balloon that trailed a guide rope through the icy waters of the Arctic Ocean and soon disappeared.

With Andree went two fellow explorers, Nils Strindberg and Knut Fraenkel. The expedition, partly financed by Alfred Nobel, the inventor of dynamite, was soon heard from when a carrier pigeon returned with a message that all was well. A letter found in a floating bouy later reported they were two days on their way, and then nothing. For thirty-three years the fate of the Andree expedition would remain a mystery, until in 1930 Norwegian explorers, visiting White Island, 300 miles east

The Andree expedition immediately after their balloon, the *Eagle*, was downed on July 11, 1897.

of Spitsbergen, discovered the frozen bodies of the three balloonists.

Wrapped in a sweater were an exposed roll of film and a pitiful diary that told of their fate—ice had formed on the gas bag and forced them down. After struggling over ice floes for more than two months they set up camp on White Island to await death. The film was carefully developed, revealing ghostly pictures of the downed balloon, of Fraenkel and Strindberg standing over a dead polar bear, and the rude camp where they finally perished.

Jules Verne, the French novelist, was inspired to write some of his most famous adventure stories as a result of discovering the 1783 balloon papers of Captain Meusnier. He found them one day in 1860 while looking through the archives in the Academy of Sciences in Paris. Meusnier had suggested a giant dirigible built with double envelopes. Verne felt there was no reason the idea wouldn't work.

He met an old friend, Felix Nadar, a noted French pioneer of photography who also shared an interest in ballooning. Nadar confided to Verne his plans to build a giant aerostat with a two-story wicker house, containing double bunks, a kitchen, dining room, even a darkroom. The thing would cost 200,000 francs, and with it Nadar hoped to raise funds to build the world's first helicopter.

The balloon, not the helicopter, intrigued Verne. He saw in his mind's eye an entire family traveling around the world in such an affair. In 1862 Verne began writing a history of ballooning, his first major work, but when he had completed it his publisher, Pierre Jules Hetzel, turned it down. "It lacks excitement, adventure!" Hetzel exclaimed. Verne got the point and agreed to a change, in return for which Hetzel signed a contract for two Jules Verne books a year for twenty years, at 20,000 francs a year. The book was a smashing success. *Five Weeks In A Balloon* was the first factual-fiction story ever written, one that would bring Verne fame and fortune. School children eagerly followed the adventures of Verne's imaginary balloonists as they floated over the deserts and jungles of Africa, from Zanzibar to Senegal, in a double-thickness balloon patterned after Meusnier's. The tale, a century later, is still hard to beat!

Nadar's balloon, *Le Géant*, turned out to be a complete success, perhaps because he ran a tight ship. Prior to departure from Paris on October 18, 1863, with nine passengers, on a record cross-country night flight, Nadar posted the following rules:

•From departure to return the captain's command shall be absolute.

•Every passenger shall declare he carries no inflammable materials.

•Silence must be absolutely observed when ordered by the captain.

•Liquors must be deposited in a common canteen, of which the captain alone has the key.

•The duration of the flight is not limited.

•All gambling is expressly prohibited.

•It is forbidden for any traveller to throw anything overboard.

•Each passenger's luggage will be limited to 30 pounds.

•It is forbidden to smoke on board.

Aboard *Le Géant* for its maiden cross-country flight were Nadar and his wife, the balloonists Etienne Mont-

A drawing of the wicker car of Felix Nadar's balloon

golfier and Jules and Luis Godard, and four others. Through the night it drifted northeastward across the Benelux countries. A number of flaming furnaces down below told the travelers they were over Belgium, as did the sound of Flemish songs rising through the night. The aerial voyagers rang bells and roared through trumpets, but received no reply.

At daylight, according to one passenger, Eugene Arnould, a reporter for the newspaper *La Nation*, they drifted low over Dutch villages in Holland, where "we distinctly saw women in their chemises look hurriedly out of windows and then rush back again. Some made the sign of the Cross." As the sun rose, the gas bag swelled dangerously under its effect, prompting Jules Godard to climb into the rigging and slash the silk with a knife, to keep from blowing out to sea. *Le Géant* came down with a crash. Arnould related the sad end of the flight:

"I jumped, and landed on my head. St. Felix was stretched on the soil frightfully disfigured; his body was one wound. He had an arm broken, his chest torn, and an ankle dislocated. I heard a cry—Nadar was stretched out on the ground with a dislocated thigh. His wife had fallen into the river. Another companion was shattered. In trying to assist Mme. Nadar, I was nearly drowned."

Aside from that, it was a fine trip.

The wreck of *le Géant*

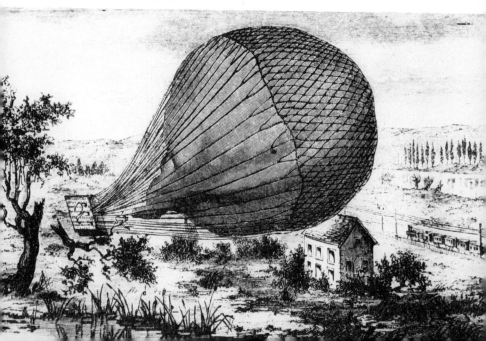

In the 1890's, a new scheme to reach the North Pole by air was proposed in Chicago by a Mt. Carmel, Illinois, inventor, Edward J. Pennington, who organized a $20,-000,000 stock company founded on a thirty-foot model dirigible, powered with an unusual three-cylinder rotary engine that ran on natural gas. The company never got off the ground, but it formed the basis for a thrilling novel titled *A Dash To The Pole*, by Herbert D. Ward, a popular pulp fiction writer.

Young readers of the Gay Nineties hid the volume inside their geography books and thrilled to Ward's description of how the thing would work: "Like a torpedo the airship shot ahead. Where could that speed stop? Twenty-five! Fifty! A hundred! Two hundred miles an hour! Faster than an eagle! Jack Hardy's hat dropped to the electrified city below. Stupified, frightened, cowed, dumb, the travellers, trembling, dared not look out. The sensation of such flight was unparalleled, uncatalogued. It was prostrating. They lost their breath. They dropped to the floor.

"The inventor, with blood-shot eyes, with the expression of a conquering god, sat at his post unmoved. He had expected this. The intoxication of success was too fine to filch his senses.

"My God!" cried Sergeant Willtwig, suddenly striking his head with both knuckles.

"What's up?" asked Professor Wilder, with a happy smile.

"I forgot the matches!"

Balloon propulsion systems occupied the minds of inventors through a good part of the nineteenth century. Before the introduction of the gasoline motor, a half-dozen powered dirigibles flew successfully. In 1852

74

Henri Giffard, a French railroad engineer, flew a 140-foot dirigible at 6 mph with a 3½-horsepower steam engine and actually proposed a bigger dirigible more than one-third mile (1,970 feet) in length.

Twenty years later a German engineer, Paul Haenlin, risked sudden death by successfully powering a round balloon with a 5½-horsepower engine that ran on hydrogen gas siphoned from the large gas bag itself. In 1883, the French brothers Albert and Gaston Tissandier built a ninety-two-foot dirigible that barely moved with a 1½-horsepower electric motor. The next year the French government financed two officers, A. C. Krebs and Charles Renard, who built a 165-foot dirigible that ran at 14 mph, pushed along by an electric motor of 8½-horsepower.

The Tissandiers' dirigible could barely move under the power of its small electric motor.

Alberto Santos-Dumont flew the first gasoline-powered dirigible on September 20, 1898.

The first dirigible to fly under gasoline power was an 82-foot sausage built by a Brazilian sportsman, Alberto Santos-Dumont. It carried a pair of engines that produced 3½-horsepower. Santos-Dumont built a dozen airships in an effort to capture a 100,000 franc prize offered by Henri Deutsch, the French gasoline king, for the first airship to leave St. Cloud, circle the Eiffel Tower, and return to land within a half hour.

One of Santos-Dumont's ships landed in a chestnut tree, and later he made a crash landing on the roof of the Trocadero. On October 19, 1901, he finally won the prize money, just twenty-nine seconds under the deadline.

The following year a Chicago inventor named Peter Samorski patented a strange airship designed like a streamlined racing yacht. It carried a gaff-rigged mainsail "to propel the vessel while in the air or while resting on the water," for weekend yachting parties that were to begin at the local marina and end up in the skies.

Simon Lake, a New Englander who invented the world's first even-keel submarine—one that submerges without diving—about this time turned to aeronautics and patented a flying submarine that operated on the same principle of bouyancy. He once explained to the author: "My 1908 airship was a compromise between the gas-filled airship and the airplane, in which I incorporated direct lifting force by a large propeller which could be swung in gimbals, so as to give an upward lift to augment the lift of the gas-filled hulls, and could then be gradually changed so as to give a forward or backward thrust in horizontal flight."

Lake's idea was a forerunner of later experimental STOL (Short Takeoff and Landing) craft that flew on the same principle of gimballed propellers, for both vertical and horizontal propulsion.

7

GRANDFATHER
OF THE
JET STREAM

Jet travelers today are aware of great stratospheric rivers of air that blow from west to east, at velocities reaching 200 miles an hour. Sweeping down from the Arctic, these air streams are responsible for much of the world's weather. Airline pilots utilize them to advantage on eastbound flights and avoid them flying west.

Called *jet streams*, these amazing upper winds were first observed and utilized by the nineteenth-century aeronaut John Wise, who penetrated the high sky in a balloon more than 450 times during a career as an airborne meteorologist that spanned four decades. In his autobiography, *Through the Air*, published one hundred years ago, Professor Wise wrote: "The great balance of nature is vibrating all the time with exact rhythmical motion; earthquakes, cyclones, and volcanos are but bars and semi-quavers in the harmony of the universe, and we, short-sighted creatures, often look upon them as catastrophes, and, with the uneducated, as the visitations of an offended Diety."

On December 20, 1843, Wise petitioned Congress for a $15,000 appropriation to construct a 100-foot exploratory balloon to plot the upper winds as a possible means of drifting swiftly from America to Europe. He told Congress: "It has been fully demonstrated that there exists in the atmosphere a constant current of wind, moving from west to east, with a velocity of more than 60 miles an hour. It is even now feasible to travel eastward with a velocity that will circumnavigate the globe in thirty to forty days . . . which would enable us to leave dispatches in Europe and China, and return by way of Oregon Territory to Washington City."

Much of Professor Wise's knowledge of meteorology came from a close friendship with Professor Joseph Henry, first secretary of the Smithsonian Institution in Washington, who in 1847 established an amazing telegraphic network that would become the basis for the United States Weather Bureau.

Professor Henry's interest in telegraphy went back many years. In 1831 he perfected the electromagnet and demonstrated he could ring a bell a mile away by pressing a button connected to a battery. This is the earliest use of the magnetic telegraph, perfected several years later by Samuel F. B. Morse.

Within a year of its founding, the Smithsonian Weather Bureau was receiving daily weather reports by telegraph from some 150 observers in all parts of the country. In 1849 Henry urged telegraph companies to open their regular morning messages by indicating general local weather conditions, instead of using the customary "O.K." signal. Thus was established the world's first system of telegraphic weather reports. District operators tapped out "fair," "rain," "cloudy," "snow," or whatever the prevailing weather, and the accumulated data were charted to track the movement of important storms. By 1850 large weather maps hung in the Smithsonian lobby, attracting great interest. The Washington *Star* printed the first daily weather forecasts in 1857, and the work load at the Smithsonian soon became so burdensome that Henry turned the project over to the War Department's Signal Service.

Professor Henry's telegraph network established conclusively the west-to-east movement of upper winds. For many years he made his weather reports available to American balloonists and took a personal interest in the increasing number of proposals for using jet streams for transoceanic flights.

On May 8, 1849, Henry wrote to Professor Wise: "I have no doubt that there are great currents in the upper regions of the atmosphere, and particularly the return currents of the trade winds, which should blow continually from southwest to northeast."

Professor Wise was already convinced. In May, 1842, he wrote in his logbook, following a balloon ascent from Bellefonte, Pennsylvania: "It is now beyond a doubt in my mind established *that a current from west to east in the atmosphere is constantly in motion* within the height of 12,000 feet above the ocean. Nearly all my trips are strong proof of this."

Professor Wise had never seen a balloon ascension when he built his first gas bag in 1835, to pursue a scientific study of meteorology. His first trip was made from

Philadelphia, scene of Blanchard's historic flight in 1793, but it was not exactly a sensation. Only half full, his balloon barely lifted him over a housetop and dropped him into a vacant lot. Wise tossed out all the ballast and his scientific instruments, but a curious crowd gathered and hung onto the basket, to see what was going on. Wise relates that he roared at the top of his voice: *"For Heaven's sake, gentlemen, will you give me a chance to make the ascension?"* Whereupon they shoved him skyward, to launch him on a career unparalleled in the history of ballooning.

On the Fourth of July, 1835, Wise soared high above the town of Lebanon, Pennsylvania, and suddenly found himself in trouble. At an altitude of three miles he discovered the valve rope broken off inside the gas bag. He had no way to come down. The balloon rose higher and higher. In desperation Wise climbed into the rigging, holding a knife in his teeth, to slash the bag open. Nausea overcame him; he couldn't reach high enough.

"I was apprehensive that it might be my last voyage," Wise recalled. In a moment he heard a sharp report— the balloon had exploded. Wise felt himself falling dizzily through the air, but as he neared earth, he noticed the bottom part of the gas bag had pushed upward, forming a crude parachute. Landing safely by tossing out the remaining ballast at the right moment, Wise thought about what had happened and made a decision. He'd try again, this time exploding the balloon on purpose!

Wise won considerable fame as a balloon-buster, and things went well until October 1, 1838, when his balloon split the wrong way, opening a seam from top to bottom. The balloon slid down the sky sideways in a wide spiral, but again he cheated death with an expert landing. Two

John Wise's balloon exploded when it rose to an altitude
above three miles but formed a crude parachute as it fell,
enabling Wise to land safely.

John Wise lost his race with William Paullin when his balloon stalled in dead air while Paullin's drifted off at high
speed.

years later he attempted to race another balloonist, William Paullin, but was chagrined when the latter drifted off at a high rate of speed while he remained stalled in dead air.

Wise later wrote down his thoughts about strange phenomena he experienced at high altitudes: "Our atmospheric shell, occupying a space between heaven and earth, is full of unexplored philosophy," he began. "Send an old wrinkled man up in a balloon three to four miles high, and he will become smoothed out like a plump faced youth. Even his old flattened eyeballs become more rotund, and this enables him to see better up there than down here. This writer can read fine print without spectacles when high up in the air, such as is blurred and illegible to his unaided eyes on earth. Not only does he see better up there, but he feels better, breathes a purer air. His blood courses more rapidly, his mind becomes exhalted." It may well have been that Wise was suffering from hypoxia (oxygen deficiency), which pilots today know can cause a sense of euphoria, or careless well-being. Wise noted something else now familiar to pilots: at a height of several miles "the earth looks like a bowl, and thus we find ourselves all the time in the center of the visible universe."

On July 1, 1859, Professor Wise made an unforgettable trial flight from St. Louis in a balloon of fifty feet diameter to check the jet-stream route, preliminary to actually establishing a balloon line from America to Europe. With him were O. A. Gager, promoter of the venture; John La Mountain, another professional balloonist; and a reporter for the St. Louis *Republican,* John Hyde.

At dusk the big balloon, christened the *Atlantic,* rose

slowly from the St. Louis Gaslight Company yards. Beneath it hung a lifeboat in a canvas sling, connected by a rope ladder. While Wise piloted the aerostat from the wicker basket alone, the other voyagers made themselves comfortable in the boat. At 6:45 P.M., as St. Louis disappeared under a pall of smoke, they broke out a bottle of champagne and a box of roast turkey.

Crossing the Mississippi driven by a strong west wind, they sailed over Illinois at 50 mph as a silvery moon rose. At 8,000 feet the *Atlantic* leveled off, and as darkness enveloped them, they were amazed to see the gas bag glow with phosphorescence, like a huge Chinese lantern. Wise wrapped himself in blankets and settled down to sleep, instructing the others to keep the balloon well up in the sky by discharging ballast if need be.

La Mountain apparently overdid it, for the *Atlantic* soon shot skyward more than two miles, forcing hydrogen gas from the balloon neck directly into Wise's face. Gager, hearing the professor gasping and gurgling in the basket above, climbed up and rescued him from certain death. "I seemed to awaken from a long sleep," Wise related, "a sleep of years, during which I dreamed of great diving-bell experiments and interplanetary balloon voyages."

Sailing through the starry night, Wise was impressed by the beauty of the scene below. Moonlight on the Wabash gave the river the appearance of a milky way, far more beautiful to him than the one above. "The sky was cloudless," he wrote in his log. "The wind upon which we were riding was one of those peculiar high barometer winds that course across our continent from west to east, carriers of tornadoes and hurricanes we experience through the hot summer months."

Wise felt uneasy. He knew from experience that such pressure systems were dangerous, and shortly after sunrise, with the *Atlantic* sailing quickly toward the shore of Lake Erie, he saw trouble coming. Sandusky, Ohio, was covered with a line of towering clouds. Wise tossed over ballast and they hurdled the cloud deck at 10,000 feet. He valved enough gas to settle back near the surface of the lake, for a monotonous voyage of 250 miles toward Buffalo. In the distance they finally spotted Niagara Falls, which to Wise resembled a "cloud factory, the sound of the plunging water like that of an aeolian harp. If not the music of the spheres," he jotted in his log, "it is at least the rhythmic language of motion."

Swinging on eastward toward Rochester, Wise put away his logbook, frowning at a rapidly advancing line of storm clouds bearing down from out of the Canadian wilderness. Today we call such weather systems *cold fronts*, and airplane pilots avoid them as dangerous, frequently loaded with particles of ice that freeze onto wings and violent turbulence that can tear an aircraft apart. Wise was well aware of the dangers, for many times he had penetrated storm clouds only to be buffeted wildly before emerging above. Quickly he valved off gas to start a descent, but as the *Atlantic* neared the ground he was shocked to see how violent the surface wind had become—trees had been snapped, fences blown away, fields of grain flattened.

All their ballast gone, Wise ordered everything loose thrown overboard. "Be prepared for the worst!" he cried. Out went the case of champagne they'd saved for the landing, Wise's valise, and all blankets and extra clothing. Gager poured a cup of wine and held it to his lips with trembling fingers, then quickly handed it to

Wise. "I can't drink it," he sobbed. Wise tossed off the wine and threw the cup into the raging storm below. He watched reporter Hyde in the boat, scribbling on a pad, "whether to make notes of the voyage or to write his last will and testament I could not tell," he admitted.

He called to Hyde and La Mountain to climb the rope ladder into the balloon car as the *Atlantic* raced out over Lake Ontario at close to 90 mph. The lifeboat slammed against the waves, threatening to throw them out. La Mountain grabbed an ax and began hacking at the boat seats, tossing them overboard.

Wise later recalled: "The storm clouds had now gathered thickly about us, and we were running low. The scene was fearfully dismal. We were between two boisterous elements. The lake was surging and foaming like a thing of wrath. The heavy clouds lashed them to a perfect fury. It seemed as though the heavens were falling down and our air-ship was endeavoring to wedge itself through."

When a steamer loomed ahead, Wise suggested they swamp the balloon and chance a rescue, but the others said no. "If we're to die," said Hyde, "let us die on land!"

For more than a hundred miles they bounced and slammed across the wild waves before the *Atlantic* thumped with a violent crash against the shoreline. Wise tossed out the iron grapnel. It snagged a tree branch and broke, and the balloon went bounding over the treetops "like a maddened elephant through a jungle." Finally the *Atlantic* hurtled into the side of a great oak and came to rest.

Just then, Wise recalled, a little old lady wearing spectacles approached, stared up at the men in the treetop and asked where they'd come from. When Wise

The *Atlantic's* lifeboat slammed against the waves of Lake Ontario as the balloon raced across the water, propelled by gale winds.

shouted "St. Louis," she clucked: "That will do, now, son!"

It was a lucky end to the longest aerial voyage ever made, more than twelve hundred miles from St. Louis to the village of Henderson, New York. The townspeople staged a big celebration, the aeronauts made speeches, and Wise led the group to the railroad station, wearing a borrowed pair of checkered pants "six inches too short." He concluded, "Thus ended the greatest balloon voyage ever made."

Professor Wise's career lasted another twenty years, before fate claimed his life on a similar voyage. He was blown over Lake Michigan in a violent storm and vanished on September 29, 1879, leaving behind an amazing record as the dean of American scientific balloonists.

8

EUROPE
OR BUST!

ASTOUNDING NEWS! BY EXPRESS VIA NORFOLK:
THE ATLANTIC CROSSED IN THREE DAYS! SIGNAL
TRIUMPH OF MR. MONCK MASON'S FLYING MA-
CHINE!

This was the startling headline that shocked the world
when the New York *Sun* hit the streets on the morning
of April 13, 1844, with a thrilling front-page story which
began:

"The great problem is at length solved! The air, as well
as the earth and the ocean, has been subdued by science
and will become a common and convenient highway
for mankind! *The Atlantic has actually been crossed in a
Balloon!*"

According to the reporter, Edgar Allan Poe, a British
balloon, the *Victoria*, had touched down at Sullivan's

A contemporary engraving shows the 44-foot model dirigible, driven by clockwork, that Monck Mason exhibited in London in 1843.

Island, near Charleston, South Carolina, after a seventy-five-hour ocean passage. Aboard were eight adventurers including the noted Monck Mason, a British aeronaut who had attracted attention the year before by exhibiting a forty-four-foot model dirigible, which flew in circles around the Royal Adelaide Gallery in London, driven by clockwork.

Mason, in 1836, had actually made a remarkable flight with Charles Green and Robert Holland in Green's huge

A poster announcing Charles Green's final night balloon ascent in the *Nassau*.

Vauxhall balloon, from Vauxhall Gardens in London to Weilburg, in the Grand Duchy of Nassau, a distance of 480 miles. The *Vauxhall*, later christened the *Nassau*, carried coal gas, a 2,000-foot drag rope, wine, parachutes for dropping messages, and a quicklime stove for brewing hot tea. Aeronaut Green was the first to propose a transatlantic balloon trip.

When Poe heard about Mason's model dirigible he was struck with a splendid idea. Stranded in Philadelphia, broke, with an ailing wife, he needed money desperately. Poe traveled to New York and delivered his amazing story to the *Sun*'s editorial offices and was delighted with the response.

"The rush for the sole paper which had the news," Poe wrote later, "was something beyond even the prodigious, and, in fact, if (as some assert) the *Victoria* did not absolutely accomplish the voyage recorded, it would be difficult to assign a reason why it should not have!"

The gullible *Sun* had also been taken in nine years before, with the celebrated "Moon Hoax." The paper published a story claiming that the British astronomer, Sir William Herschel, had built a great telescope in Africa capable of seeing men on the moon, and it was Poe who had then tried to expose the deception. Today, of course, men have been to the moon, and interestingly, in 1919 the British Army dirigible R-34, the first airship to cross the Atlantic, made its return trip in just four minutes less time than Poe assigned to Mason's nonexistent *Victoria* seventy-five years before.

One man greatly amused by Poe's balloon hoax was old Phineas T. Barnum, a showman who started his career in 1835 by exhibiting a reputedly 161-year-old black woman named Joice Heth, who claimed she had been little George Washington's nurse.

Barnum took an interest in aeronautics when he toured Europe with his famed midget, Tom Thumb. At the Surrey Zoological Gardens, General Tom Thumb delighted British children by ascending in a tiny balloonet, part of an unsuccessful British dirigible built by two Swiss inventors, Samuel John Pauley and Durs Egg, known as *Egg's Folly*.

Back in America, influenced by the Poe story, Barnum offered $5,000 to the first man who would fly the Atlantic, but quickly withdrew the offer when an anonymous aeronaut was said to have accepted the challenge.

In 1858 a rival balloonist to America's renowned scientific aeronaut, John Wise, appeared on the scene. Professor Carlincourt made his first ascent from Ottawa to help celebrate the completion of Cyrus Field's first transatlantic submarine telegraph cable. When Carlincourt began construction of a transatlantic balloon in Hoboken, New Jersey, Professor Wise denounced him publicly as an "unscrupulous plagiarist" and "a magician by profession."

Professor Carlincourt, whose real name was Thaddeus Sobieski Constantine Lowe, was trying hard to raise money for his Atlantic flight. He gave scientific lecture tours, in which he filled soap bubbles with hydrogen gas and sent them floating to the ceiling.

Thaddeus Lowe, in fact, gave full credit to Wise for discovery of the upper wind system and plunged ahead building his big balloon, the *City of New York*, with a capacity of 725,000 cubic feet of coal gas. When the Manhattan Gas Works failed to deliver the coal gas at a fast enough rate, Lowe moved his project to Philadelphia.

Sponsored by Dr. John C. Cresson, president of the Franklin Institute and owner of the Point Breeze Gas Works, Lowe finally completed his airship and renamed

Thaddeus Lowe, the top-hatted man in front center, supervises the inflation of his airship *Great Western*.

it the *Great Western*. It made only one flight, with Cresson and four other passengers on board, coming down in a Jersey mud flat. The fabric had not withstood rough handling on the move from New York.

Lowe sought counsel from Professor Joseph Henry of the Smithsonian, who advised him to try out the wind system on a flight from Cincinnati eastward, before venturing over the open sea. On April 19, 1861, Lowe ascended from Cincinnati in a small balloon, the *Enterprise*, on a historic flight to Pea Ridge, South Carolina.

He made the trip in top hat and tails, carrying a napkin of cookies, having been called from a banquet at midnight when a fresh west wind sprang up.

The Civil War was on—Fort Sumter had been fired on the week before—and when Lowe landed, carrying abolitionist newspapers from Cincinnati, he was arrested as a Yankee spy, the first prisoner of war in that bloody conflict, but was soon released.

Lowe gave up plans for transatlantic ballooning and offered his services to President Abraham Lincoln, becoming head of the Union Army's first Aeronautic Corps, a story told in the chapter on war balloons. With the Civil War and with the deaths of Professor Wise and Washington Harrison Donaldson, both drowned in Lake Michigan while ballooning, efforts to reach Europe by riding the westerly winds ended until after the turn of the century. Donaldson, a balloonist with Barnum's

Lowe's transatlantic balloon gear included grapnels, floats, and a mail pouch.

This photograph of Walter Wellman's dirigible *America* was taken from the *Trent*.

Traveling Hippodrome, had also dreamed of a transatlantic flight, and once actually got as far as New Canaan, Connecticut, en route from Brooklyn to Paris in 1873.

In 1910, a daring American journalist, Walter Wellman, set sail from Atlantic City for Europe in a dirigible, the *America*, with five companions and a grey kitten as mascot. The airship carried the first airborne wireless radio, but all Wellman could report was trouble. Only 140 miles northeast of Nantucket Island, northerly winds howled down to blow Wellman far off course. He radioed a passing liner, the *Trent*, which took the crew off the *America* 375 miles out from Norfolk, Virginia. The airship was abandoned.

Shortly before World War I a westward crossing of the Atlantic was planned in a 500,000-cubic foot balloon, the *Suchard*, utilizing the trade winds, but the flight was canceled at the last moment due to technical difficulties. Not until well after World War II, with the development of new materials and new techniques, was the Atlantic once more braved by balloon, again from east to west.

In mid-December, 1958, one of the most remarkable transatlantic balloon attempts on record began when a party of four adventurers—three men and a woman—left tiny Tenerife in the Canary Islands, hoping to reach the West Indies by riding the easterly trade winds. Theirs was an epic adventure of courage and stamina, and they

An engraving shows the elaborate balloon in which John Wise and Washington Harrison Donaldson had planned to cross the Atlantic.

were defeated only by a wild storm like those that took the lives of Wise and Donaldson.

Their balloon, the *Small World*, was a marvel of scientific ingenuity, constructed of a synthetic fiber coated with neoprene plastic, light and durable, forty-six feet in diameter. Slung beneath it was a nicely engineered gondola boat of reinforced styrene. In it they carried supplies and emergency equipment designed for their 2,700-mile sea journey.

Their gear included 200 pounds of food concentrate, twenty gallons of fresh water, and solar stills with which to manufacture drinking water from ocean water. They also carried a supply of calcium hydride, which forms fresh hydrogen gas when combined with sea water, plus an assortment of navigational and meteorological instruments, and a bugle for a foghorn.

The balloonists were Arnold Eiloart, his son Tim, Colin Mudie, and his wife Rosemary, all four British subjects. None had ballooning experience before their project got under way, but all quickly qualified as experts.

Following a harrowing liftoff in a rising gale they soared westward, and for a time the trip was uneventful. They carried a drag rope, invented by their countryman, Charles Green, but added something new—a water bucket with which to scoop up sea water for ballast, at the end of a 3,000-foot line.

On the third day out, they were driven beneath a towering thunderhead that reared like a giant stalk of cauliflower into the blue sky. Underneath, all was black and menacing. They were caught in the rising current of air, which they knew could carry them to their deaths at 30,000 feet, where there is virtually no oxygen to breathe. By quickly valving off hydrogen they slowed their ascent and finally emerged beyond the dangerous column of rising air.

After traveling 1,200 nautical miles, half way to the New World, they encountered another, more severe thunderstorm whose convective current hurtled them skyward with such ferocity that Tim scrambled into the rigging and tore at the balloon's neck to keep it from exploding. Higher and higher they rose, in the blackness, pelted by rain and hailstones, until nearly a mile above the sea they found equilibrium.

They'd valved off too much gas, to avert disaster in the storm clouds, and there had been no time to renew it. Overboard went everything loose, as the canopy flapped wildly overhead. Down they came, plunging free of the cloud base barely above the waves. As the boat struck, they cut away the balloon and watched it vanish in the darkness.

They had been aloft 94½ hours—an unofficial world record—but the West Indies still lay half an ocean away. After rigging a sail and fitting a rudder to their little boat, they set off to complete the epic voyage and reached Barbados in good shape.

Theirs would not be the last attempt at an Atlantic crossing by balloon. In 1968 Mark Winters and Jerry Kostur, a pair of professional movie stuntmen, set off for Europe from Halifax, Nova Scotia, riding a fifteen-foot plastic sailboat slung beneath a 35,000-cubic foot balloon, christened the *Maple Leaf*. They carried twelve gallons of fresh water and survival rations, but fifty miles out they were becalmed. A fishing boat rescued them.

A tragic attempt to reach the elusive goal took place in September, 1970, when the *Free Life*, a balloon eighty feet high and fifty feet in diameter, gaily banded in orange with yellow and white stripes, sailed away from a Long Island meadow with three adventurers on board. They were Malcolm Brighton, an experienced, thirty-two-year-old British aeronaut, Rodney Anderson, a commodities broker of the same age, and his wife, Pamela.

Like so many aeronauts before them, they depended on the westerly wind system to waft them to Europe; they hoped to reach France within a week. Their ascension was witnessed by residents of a nearby art colony, close to East Hampton. A reporter for the *New York Times* saw them toss out ballast from their twelve-foot gondola and sail away "like a fancy basketball dribble, culminating in a hop, skip, and jump across a country fence, as a thousand persons cheered."

The *Free Life*, similar in form to the unlucky Rozier's Charlo-Montgolfier, was a combination balloon, inflated not with hydrogen and "phlogiston" but hot air and non-inflammable helium. Their flight profile called for leveling off at 8,000 feet, where fifty-knot winds were reported. The cost of the venture, more than $100,000, was borne by Anderson's father-in-law. The expenses of the journey were to be recovered by carrying special envelopes to commemorate the journey.

All went well at first. As other balloonists before them, they carried "survival" gear—champagne, cognac, food, a guitar, five pounds of books, cameras, a rifle, a machete, a portable toilet, a radio, water, and a propane stove.

Anderson told reporters he was inspired to make the trip by Salomon August Andree, the balloonist who was lost in the frozen north in an effort to reach the pole. Brighton had twice crossed the English Channel by balloon.

From time to time, radio messages were received from the *Free Life*, reporting everything normal. Then twenty-nine hours out, a frantic call was heard: *"Six hundred feet and descending . . . signing off . . . will try contact after landing!"*

What happened may never be known. The vast expanse of ocean and the sky above it holds the secret to many disappearances, most traceable to freak weather situations caused by interaction of the sea and the atmosphere. Today we are only beginning to understand this relationship, from observations made by orbiting satellites and jet aircraft that fly high above the ocean weather factory.

Crossing the Atlantic by balloon continues to be a challenge, and perhaps one day someone will succeed. As this book was written in 1973, Professor Wise's old dream was renewed by a group of adventurers, called Jet Stream Expeditions. They hope to cross the Atlantic with a giant, 500,000-cubic foot, hot-air balloon 101 feet in diameter.

With space-age technology, George Stokes, Dave Burt, and Dr. James Lamont Wright believe they can succeed where others have failed. Their plan is to ascend to stratospheric heights, between 35,000 and 40,000 feet, where jet stream cores exist, and to cross the ocean at a speed of 100 knots or more.

Stokes, a veteran of more than 550 ascensions in nearly a decade of ballooning, believes much scientific knowledge of the stratosphere can be gained from this flight, which he does not consider a stunt. Yet he shares the romantic dreams of the early aeronauts. (Stokes once built and flew a 60,000 cubic foot replica of Vincent Lunardi's 1783 balloon, the first to ascend from England.) But instead of pumping away with silken oars, he plans to carry aboard scientific gear and space equipment developed for America's astronauts.

9

WAR
BALLOONS

Balloons have played an important role in warfare for more than a century and were seriously considered for both offensive and defensive combat from the very birth of aerostation. After watching the first humans go up in a Montgolfier in 1783, Benjamin Franklin prophetically suggested their use for military reconnaissance, for signaling, and for lifting sieges. Within ten years military ballooning was an accomplished fact.

The first company of French *aerostiers* was created under Col. Jean-Marie-Joseph Coutelle on April 2, 1794, at a military Aeronautic School at Meudon, near Paris. Assisting Colonel Coutelle was Guyton de Morveau, a French chemist. Four balloons thirty-two feet in diameter were built to train the initial class of fifty military pilots, who were raised on ropes 600 feet to practice

Colonel Coutelle observed combat conditions from the *Entrepenant* during the battle of Fleurus—the first military use of balloons.

reconnaissance. The *Entrepenant, Celeste, Hercule,* and *Intrepide* would see action in various sectors, at a time when most of Europe was united against the French Republican Government.

In June, 1794, Colonel Coutelle made history's first ascent under combat conditions from Mauberge, 125 miles northeast of Paris, in the *Entrepenant.* Prior to the battle of Fleurus, with two other officers along, he twice rose several thousand feet and stayed aloft four hours on each ascension, coming down amidst a hail of cannon-fire. The information he gathered helped France win a decisive victory over Austrian forces. Napoleon used balloon observers during his siege of Mantua in Italy, in 1797, and the following year moved a balloon corps to Egypt, where the equipment was captured by the enemy.

In America, the first use of balloons in warfare was proposed in 1840 by Col. John H. Shelburne, who appealed to Secretary of War Joel R. Poinsett to outfit the United States Army with observation balloons for the Seminole Indian campaign in Florida. Charles Durant, the first American aeronaut, had just retired, but offered to sell his old balloon to the army for $600. Before action was taken the campaign ended.

The American Civil War was the real proving ground for reconnaissance balloons. The man who put them to test was Professor Thaddeus Lowe, whose friendship with Professor Joseph Henry of the Smithsonian won him an audience with President Lincoln. Lowe staged a demonstration ascension from the Columbian Armory in Washington, and on this historic occasion took with him two telegraphers. Equipment was connected by wire with the President's house and the War Department. On the morning of June 18, 1861, Lowe dictated the following telegram, the first ever sent from the sky:

Balloon Enterprise
In The Air
June 18, 1861

To His Excellency Abraham Lincoln, President of the United States.

Dear Sir:

From this point of observation we command an extent of country nearly fifty miles in diameter. I have the pleasure of sending you this first telegram ever dispatched from an aerial station, and acknowledging indebtedness to your encouragement for the opportunity of demonstrating the availability of the science of aeronautics in the service of the country. I am, your excellency's obedient servant.

T. S. C. Lowe

Lincoln watched thoughtfully from his window and summoned Lowe for a chat, which ran well past midnight. The next morning Lowe left the White House with Lincoln's endorsement. Within a month he was on active duty, but as a civilian aeronaut. In late July Confederate troops were swarming toward Washington and Federal troops were in full retreat after Bull Run. Gen. George B. McClellan, in command of the defense army, desperately needed information on the Rebels' avenues of attack. Lowe ascended with the *Enterprise* and observed the enemy troops between Manassas Junction and Fairfax, then put aside his spy glass, tossed out ballast, and began a free flight back toward Arlington. Descending once more, he was greeted by small arms fire—from Federal troops. With no flag aboard he dared not risk further descent, so again rose and sailed away over Secessia, coming down well behind Rebel lines.

Lowe's pretty wife, Leontine, saved the day. She appealed to the 31st New York Volunteers to send out scouts and locate her husband, then disguised herself as a farm woman and led a horse and wagon through

the woods to where Thad was concealed. They hurriedly piled the balloon into the wagon and covered it with straw, and Lowe hid underneath while his wife drove through the lines to safety.

In December 1861, Lowe had seven balloons operating. Largest were the *Union* and her twin, the *Intrepid*, both of 32,000 cubic feet capacity. The others were the *Constitution*, *Washington*, *Eagle*, and *Excelsior*. His Balloon Corps included a number of former circus balloon-

This photo shows Lowe preparing to ascend in the *Enterprise* to observe enemy troops between Manassas Junction and Fairfax during the Civil War.

ists, including William Paullin, James and Ezra Allen, John Steiner, and John B. Starkweather. John Wise served briefly with the Topographical Bureau as Lowe's rival, until his balloon was mistakenly shot down by Union troops as a Rebel machine.

Operating from Cairo, Illinois, with the Western Department, Steiner complained to Lowe that "I can not git eny ascistence here. Thay say thay know nothing about my balloon business thay even laugh ad me. Let me hear from you as soon as possible and give me a paper from Headquarters to show theas blockheads hoo I am! All the officers hear are as dum as a set of asses."

In April, 1861, balloonist Starkweather went south to assist in the blockade of Port Royal, South Carolina, and made a number of ascents from the "world's first aircraft carrier", the steamer *Mayflower*, observing Rebel activity in and around Savannah. Starkweather moved his operations closer to Charleston the next month, and made further reconnaissance ascensions in his balloon, the *Washington*.

Lowe's proudest moment came during the Battle of Fair Oaks, a bloody engagement that took a toll of 10,000 Americans, dead or wounded, on both sides. McClellan's Army of the Potomac had placed Richmond, the Rebel capital, under siege, but spring rains in '62 flooded the Chickahominy River, dividing his army. Gen. Joseph E. Johnson's defending army, aware of this, in the night gathered strength for a crushing blow, to turn the siege into a rout.

Lowe had by now perfected his field gas generator. He could quickly inflate his balloons for emergency flights, by pouring sulphuric acid over scrap iron in a zinc-lined army wagon and passing the gas through a hose joined to the balloon neck. The hose was connected to a pump which gave trouble because it frosted over when the gas expanded, causing the valve to stick.

McClellan called Lowe to his field tent and asked the aeronaut to ascend at daybreak from Mechanicsville.

"Have a good look at the road from Seven Pines," he ordered. "If they move up from there we're in for trouble!"

Lowe swung into his saddle and rode through the rainy night to his balloon outpost, where the *Constitution* tugged at her ropes behind a clump of maples, fully inflated. He stepped into the basket and signaled to ascend. At 800 feet he scanned the horizon. Rebel wagons churned along the muddy road from Seven Pines, followed by black lines of men, marching. "Down!" he yelled through cupped hands. "Fast!"

Lowe sprinted to the telegrapher's tent and shook awake the operator, Park Spring. "Send this to McClellan, fast!" he snapped. He handed Spring a hastily scribbled note, which the telegrapher immediately tapped out: "There are large bodies of troops in the open field beyond the open heights on the New Bridge Road. White covered wagons are rapidly moving toward the point of engagement, with artillery in advance. The firing on our left has ceased. T. S. C. Lowe, Chief Aeronaut."

The siege of Richmond was now a battle for survival by the Union forces. McClellan needed desperately to join his forces, if they could find some way to cross the Chickahominy. Spring's instrument began clicking, and in a moment he turned to Lowe: "The General wants you to take me up and keep a running account of the battle. Can you do it?"

Lowe frowned. The *Constitution* could not lift both men, and the big *Intrepid* was only half inflated. Without a word Lowe hurried to the *Intrepid* and studied it. He grabbed a tea kettle from a camp fire and knocked the bottom out. He shouted to his startled men to bring over the *Constitution*. With their help he connected the *Con-*

Lowe and a telegrapher went aloft in the *Intrepid* to report on the Battle of Fair Oaks. In this picture only the basket of the balloon is visible as soldiers let out the anchoring ropes.

stitution's neck to the *Intrepid*, using the tea kettle for a funnel. The men pulled down on the *Constitution's* netting, and within minutes the *Intrepid* was bulging.

Lowe and his telegrapher rose to 1,000 feet, paying out the copper wire. Spyglass to his eye, he slowly dictated history's first running account of a major engagement sent from an aerial post.

At headquarters, General McClellan chomped hard on his cigar, grabbing Lowe's messages in short takes from his key man. In between he snapped orders to his aides. Somehow the threatened Union Army regrouped over tiny, shaking Grapevine Bridge, located by Lowe. His balloon reports saved the day and stopped a desperate Confederate attack that could well have rolled clear to Washington and changed history.

For Lowe, there was disappointment. He contracted fever from his service in the swamps and retired from military life. Afterward, he remembered the frost on the gas valve and patented a gas process based on it for artificial refrigeration. With that, and a similar patented process for making artificial gas, he built a fortune and retired to Pasadena, California, where he founded the Pasadena Gas Works.

At the turn of the century Professor Lowe, an old man, once more turned his eyes skyward. He bought a mountain and named it for himself—Mount Lowe—and there established a weather station to study the unusual meteorology of Southern California, with the idea of starting up a balloon airline to Las Vegas with a giant craft resembling his original transatlantic balloon and called the *Lowe Planet Airship*. Death took him before the new ship was built.

Forgotten by historians were activities of the Confederate Air Force during the Civil War. They began during the Peninsular Campaign, when Gen. Joseph E. Johnston brought a cotton hot-air balloon from Richmond to counter activities of the Union Aeronautic Corps. The balloonist was Capt. John Randolph Bryan, a Virginia calvary officer, who made the mistake of volunteering for a special mission, unaware it involved sky duty.

Bryan made three ascents in the cotton balloon, on the last accidentally breaking away for a thrilling free flight over enemy lines. Snipers fired at him but missed. Bryan's balloon came down over the York River, and to save himself he tossed overboard a fine pair of boots. The wind shifted, blowing him to shore, and he made his way barefoot to headquarters with important information on Union positions.

Later, during the siege of Richmond, Professor Lowe was surprised to see another balloon on the horizon. This one was made of gaily colored silk provided by a Charleston merchant, E. L. Kerrison, and inflated with city gas at Richmond. Bryan served the Confederacy well during the battle of Gaines Mill, but on July 4, 1863, the silk balloon, tied aboard a small tug, the *Teaser*, on the James River, was captured by a Federal gunboat, the *Maritanza*. The ornate balloon was taken to Washington and cut into small pieces for souvenirs for members of Congress. "And there went the last silk dress in the Confederacy," a Southern officer sighed.

One of the most remarkable uses of balloons in warfare occurred during the Franco-Prussian War, when they were employed to maintain contact between besieged Paris and the provinces. From September 23, 1870, to January 28, 1871, sixty-two balloons were manufactured inside Parisian railroad stations and sent aloft. Only six were captured by the Germans, and two were blown to sea.

More than one hundred persons escaped from Paris by balloon, and fifty-four aerostats were used to dispatch 2,500,000 air mail letters, whose weight totaled four tons. Some balloons took along carrier pigeons, to which microscopic photographs of the London *Times* were attached, beneath the middle tail feather. In an hour or

Le Neptune was the first of sixty-two balloons built to counteract the Siege of Paris. Felix Nadar photographed it leaving the Place St. Pierre on September 23, 1870, for Evreux carrying 227 pounds of letters.

two they returned to Paris, where the microphotographs were blown up on a screen by a magic lantern. Reporters made copies which were printed in the evening Parisian papers.

Felix Nadar, Eugene and Jules Godard, Gaston and Albert Tissandier were among the patriots who rallied to the tricolor and built and flew war balloons for France. Biggest was *La Liberté*, of 176,000 cubic feet, which broke away during inflation on October 18, 1870, and fell inside Prussian lines in Le Bourget. Nadar provided a note of high drama when, after setting up a balloon shuttle service between Paris and Tours, he attempted to enter the city by the aerial route. He encountered a German balloonist at the city's outskirts and both opened fire with rifles—history's first aerial battle.

Completed too late for use during the Siege of Paris was a giant dirigible balloon built by a distinguished naval architect, Stanislas-Charles Henri-Laurent Dupuy de Lome, who built the first steam warships. With no steam engine available, he installed a four-bladed propeller, fitted to a crankshaft to be turned by eight passengers.

Observation balloons also played a role in Cuba during the Spanish-American War. On June 30, 1898, balloonist Ivy Baldwin ascended before Santiago de Cuba and confirmed rumors that Admiral Cervera's fleet lay at anchor in the harbor. During World War I, captive balloons were modified into streamlined bags that could withstand winds up to 50 miles an hour. These were designated "Balloons, Limp," or "Blimps." Best was the French Caquot type, able to ride out a seventy-mph gale. In World War II captive balloons served to raise steel-cable barrages over British cities and ships at sea, forcing planes to fly too high for bombing accuracy.

Dupuy de Lome's dirigible was designed to be powered by its eight passengers.

When the allies landed in France during World War II, balloon barrages were used to protect the ships from low-flying enemy strafers.

One of the strangest uses of war balloons was the launching from Japan, in World War II of more than a thousand Fugo balloons, unmanned aerostats carrying bombs, with special devices that held them drifting at altitudes where the jet streams blew. A number of these actually reached North America, but a news blackout kept the Japanese from knowing they had succeeded, and they were abandoned as ineffectual.

U.S. Navy officers inspect a captured Fugo balloon at Moffett Field, California.

10

HOTELS
IN THE SKY

Most remarkable of all lighter-than-air craft were the giant rigid dirigibles that prowled the skies during the first three decades of this century. These monsters claimed an ancestry almost as ancient as that of spheroidal balloons. The first dirigible was proposed in 1783 by Capt. J. B. M. Meusnier, as related earlier, but the grandfather of the rigids was the Prussian Count Ferdinand von Zeppelin, whose name remains closely associated with this type of airship.

Conceived in peace but later converted to wartime use, Zeppelins were mighty machines that served as airborne hotels, transporting people in luxury across land and sea at an unhurried pace. Of 157 rigid airships actually built, 138 were manufactured in Germany. Count von Zeppelin was sixty-two in 1900 when he started off the new century by completing *Luftschiff Zeppelin No. 1*, after announcing: "I intend to build a vessel which will be able to travel to places which cannot be approached by other means of transportation, and for observation of hostile fleets and armies, *but not for active participation in actual warfare.* My dirigible balloon must be able to travel for several days without renewing provisions, gas, or fuel."

Zeppelin was born at Lake Constance, where in 1899 he built a huge floating hangar for the LZ-1, a giant cigar-shaped dirigible 420 feet long containing 400,000 cubic feet of hydrogen gas. LZ-1 was hardly a success. It lifted its calculated load, but its primitive engine and steering rudders failed. It struggled upward 400 meters, then was wrecked on landing.

Count Ferdinand von Zeppelin's floating hangar on Lake Constance housed the LZ-1, a huge cigar-shaped dirigible that was wrecked on landing after its first ascent.

The Graf, as von Zeppelin was called, had come to America in 1863 and served as a volunteer observer with the Union Army, making one balloon ascension from a training field at Fort Snelling, Minnesota. Later he began experimenting with dirigible balloons, in 1784, eventually developing his "Zeps" for the German postal service.

The Graf was not unmindful of the military potential of his rigid aircraft. In America a number of similar proposals had been made, such as a strange "Aerial Train" made up of a number of joined cylinders designed by Capt. Carl W. Petersen, a San Francisco master mariner. Petersen formed a $100,000 stock company in New York in 1885. He called attention to the versatility of his airship, which could be made longer or shorter simply by adding or subtracting segments. It was, he pointed out, remarkably suited to bombing cities from the sky.

In the same year the public was shocked by a proposed "Dynamite Balloon" invented by Russell Thayer of Philadelphia. This was to be a craft 185 feet long propelled by a jet of compressed air and sheathed in aluminum. The Army Ordnance Board recommended building a Dynamite Balloon 367 feet long, but the plan was abandoned.

Other unusual dirigibles were proposed, some were granted patents, but none flew. Among them was a two-story flying hotel to be elevated by two cigar-shaped balloons, the invention of Levi Beardsley of Dodge City, Kansas. Another was a fantastic flying vacuum bottle invented by Dr. Arthur De Bausset of Chicago, who formed a $10,000,000 corporation, the Transcontinental Aerial Navigation Company, in 1886. Nothing came of it.

To Joseph H. Dillon-Gregg of St. Louis, the answer to

the dirigible problem lay in fitting the whole thing with spiral fins and rotating it with a chain-drive so it would bore its way through the air. Again, a flop.

Nicholas Borgfeldt, a Brooklyn traveling salesman, tried very hard in 1889 to sell his patented idea of a dirigible rowed through the air by a crew of six men, much in the manner of de Lome's French aerostat, but he just wasn't a good enough salesman to put the plan over.

One more inventor made headlines in 1894, with publication of a patented scheme for blasting a giant airliner through the sky at 200 miles an hour, by exploding nitroglycerin capsules behind it every five seconds. The inventor, Dr. Edwin Pynchon, a Chicago eye, ear, nose, and throat doctor, failed as a sky-chariot designer, but succeeded in developing a widely-used speculum, with which to examine inflamed nostrils.

During the early 1900s American balloonists like Ed Unger, Ivy Baldwin, Roy Knabenshue, and Capt. Thomas

Roy Knabenshue, one of America's most active balloonists during the early 1900s, toured the country by dirigible.

Scott Baldwin kept aerostation alive. Elongated balloons raced each other through the sky like great rubber cows, and Knabenshue toured the country taking up a dozen people at a time, for thrill rides over the old home town.

But it was Count von Zeppelin who inaugurated regular airship service with his huge rigid craft, when in 1909 he finally built one that worked well. Seventy-one years old, the Graf formed the Deutsche Luftschiffahrts-Aktien-Gesellschaft—better known as *Delag*—an airline company offering both pleasure and commercial transportion through German skies. In five years prior to the outbreak of World War I, his fleet of Zeps made 1,600 safe flights, carrying 37,250 passengers without injury.

During the war years, the Graf turned to military pro-

duction of eighty-eight Zeppelins, which operated under both the German Army and Navy for North Sea patrol, scouting, and raids against England. By the war's end they had grown to 2,400,000 cubic feet, flew at 80 mph and could lift fifty tons of bombs to more than 20,000 feet altitude. They carried machine gun positions in the cars and atop the hull, and could lower a bombardier at the end of a cable, through a cloud layer, to direct raids.

After the war Germany built the LZ-126 as war reparations payment to the United States. She was rechristened the *Los Angeles* and flown across the Atlantic in October, 1924. Still bigger was the *Graf Zeppelin*, of 3,708,600 cubic feet, completed in 1928. She made an amazing total of 590 flights, including 144 ocean crossings, carrying more than 13,000 passengers before being

Count von Zeppelin inaugurated regular airship service with his first successful dirigible.

decommissioned in 1937. The Count's successor, Hugo Eckner, piloted her around the world on a 21,700-mile flight in 20 days 4 hours in 1929.

In all, the United States had four rigid aircraft—the *Los Angeles*, the *Shenandoah*, a Zeppelin copy, and the *Akron* and *Macon*, both built in this country by the Goodyear Zeppelin Corporation (now Goodyear Aerospace Corporation). Of those four airships, only the *Los Angeles* survived disaster. Despite the glamor and apparent safety of these big craft, they were no match for the storm gods when weather went on a rampage, even when filled with non-inflammable helium.

A shocking series of airship catastrophes began in 1922 when the *Roma*, an Italian-built semi-rigid U.S. Navy craft, struck high tension wires near Langley Field, Virginia, and burst into flames that took thirty-three lives. Eleven men jumped to safety. Hydrogen was never again used in American dirigibles.

The Navy's first American-built dirigible, the ZR-1, was christened the *Shenandoah*. In the summer of 1925 she was sent on a good-will tour to build confidence in airships. Ironically, it was on this trip that she bucked into a line squall over Marietta, Ohio, on September 3, 1925, was shoved skyward more than 3,000 feet in wild turbulence, and ripped apart in midair. All but the forward section of the *Shenandoah* plunged to earth, killing fourteen men, including her skipper, Comdr. Zachary Lansdowne. Lieut. Comdr. Charles Rosendahl heroically rode the nose section down safely, piloting it as a free balloon.

Bad luck continued. In 1928, Gen. Umberto Nobile's dirigible *Italia* crashed on Arctic ice returning from a trip over the Pole, but he was eventually rescued with his crew. Two years later the British dirigible *R-101*,

The U.S. Navy dirigible *Akron* during construction

headed for India, crashed in flames in France, killing all but six aboard. The *Akron* (ZRS-4), completed in 1931, was flown some 1,200 hours until she encountered a severe storm off the New Jersey coast on April 4, 1933, and crashed with a loss of seventy-three lives, including Adm. William A. Moffett.

Coincidentally, the Navy's huge *Akron* was the second airship of that name to meet disaster. In 1912 a privately-owned *Akron* left Atlantic City, New Jersey, for a transatlantic hop, but shortly after takeoff caught fire and was destroyed. Her owner, Melville Vaniman, and four others perished.

Sistership to the Navy *Akron* was the *Macon*, launched in 1933 and assigned to west coast duty at Sunnyvale, California. Returning from fleet maneuvers on February

12, 1935, the *Macon* encountered severe turbulence that collapsed her upper fin, resulting in loss of control. She sank slowly in the sea off the California coast. All crew members were rescued, but two, who jumped too soon.

Aside from the hazard of hydrogen gas, which took its deadly toll over the years, since the death of Pilatre de Rozier in 1785, the giant-killer was weather, as it is today with heavier-than-air machines. It was one thing to ride out a fast-moving cold front in a pear-shaped balloon at express-train speed, but quite another to be trapped in rushing vertical winds beneath a building thunderstorm. Such convective currents imposed relentless shear loads that dirigibles simply were not stressed to resist.

Queen of the rigids was the great LZ-129 *Hindenburg*, an 803-foot Zeppelin of 7,063,000 cubic feet, ruggedly constructed around thirty-six longitudinal girders and fifteen wire-braced main traverse frames. She was powered with four 1,100-hp Mercedes-Benz diesel engines and cruised at 78 mph. Carrying seventy passengers in complete luxury, her range was 8,750 miles.

The *Hindenburg* inaugurated history's first commercial air service across the Atlantic, in 1936 carrying 1,002 passengers on ten scheduled round trips between Germany and the United States. Average crossing times were sixty-five hours eastbound, and fifty-two hours westbound, by flying pressure patterns. These circuitous flights caused some people to believe they were deliberate wanderings, to enable Nazi spies on board to map America's east coast.

A flight aboard the *Hindenburg* was an unforgettable experience, for those who cared to spend $400 to cross the Atlantic in two days, compared to a week aboard an

A 1936 poster urged travelers to fly across the Atlantic on the *Hindenburg*.

Now.. FLY TO EUROPE!

HINDENBURG

D-LZ129

Via **AIRSHIP "HINDENBURG"** *And* **AMERICAN AIRLINES** INC.

ocean liner. On May 6, 1936, she inaugurated trans-oceanic service, and on the same day American Airlines began a coast-to-coast connecting service. Passengers could leave Los Angeles aboard a DC-3 skysleeper and arrive fresh in New York the next morning, to be flown to nearby Lakehurst, New Jersey, for the crossing.

There were two berths in each stateroom aboard the *Hindenberg*, with all comforts provided—hot and cold running water, downy beds, shower baths, steward service. A modern electric kitchen prepared 300 gourmet meals daily. In addition, passengers could enjoy a writing room, lounge, and bar, with a wide gallery and promenade deck on either side. These facilities were tucked inside the hull, not suspended below it.

Departures were made at 10 P.M. from Lakehurst. The giant airship cruised silently and smoothly, north over New York City's blaze of lights, then followed the coast up over New England and Newfoundland, before crossing the North Atlantic.

Passengers in the lounge could amuse themselves by gazing directly down through a plate glass window at the unfolding panorama below, watching the huge, cigar-shaped shadow slither across the miles. Others gathered around an aluminum piano, to sing at history's first flying piano bar.

Because the *Hindenburg* carried hydrogen gas, the smoking room and bar were pressurized, to avoid an explosion. The electric kitchen was similarly designed. Originally the *Hindenburg* was meant to carry helium, an inert gas with 93% the lifting power of hydrogen, but completely safe. However, the only helium gas fields of consequence were in Texas, New Mexico, Kansas, and Utah, hence the German Zeppelin works could not ob-

The *Hindenburg* disaster brought dirigible travel to an end.

tain it, when the United States placed an embargo on its shipment to Nazi Germany.

On May 4, 1937, the giant dirigible left Germany for Lakehurst, poked its silvery nose through the ocean mists for two days and nights, and arrived at the naval lighter-than-air base toward evening of May 6. On hand to greet the *Hindenburg* was a cub reporter from the New York *Herald-Tribune*, Ansel Talbert, who arrived late. Talbert hurried to a phone in the Navy hangar and called his city desk, to let them know he'd arrived.

At that moment he glanced out the window, watching the silvery giant nosing against the mooring mast. "There was a sudden brilliance and the airship was circled with a smoke ring," Talbert remembered. "Then the whole thing was engulfed in flames."

Talbert gasped out the news to his shocked editor and scored a news beat over the veteran newsmen, outside on the ramp. Amazingly, sixty-one persons of ninety-seven on board survived the holocaust. The *Hindenburg* disaster was never fully explained, though two theories emerged. Either a spark of static electricity touched off the explosion just as the ship reached the mooring mast, or a saboteur was responsible. Whatever the cause, the tragedy spelled the end of an era.

Today jet aircraft whisk passengers coast to coast or overseas at near sonic speeds, and supersonic transports have been built capable of flying at twice the speed of sound. Yet there are those who still believe in helium-filled dirigibles, that can serve as virtual hotels in the sky, cruising leisurely over mountains and deserts and oceans as the big rigids once did, before the *Hindenburg* tragedy brought it all to an end.

11

GHOST
BALLOONS

Of all the uses for ballooning, its role in man's quest for scientific knowledge has been most rewarding. He lives at the bottom of an atmospheric sea where strange and often frightening phenomena occur. Thunder and lightning, tornadoes and hurricanes, devastating floods and droughts are born far above in the upper world. Before balloons, man could only guess what lay above him.

Benjamin Franklin did his best, tying a key to a kite tail to lure lightning bolts from clouds, but scientific meteorology really began with the first hydrogen balloon ascent in 1783. Monsieur Charles, the balloonist, was also a prominent physicist, and showed the value of ballooning by taking along a barometer, to measure the pressure drop as the balloon rose. He read the maximum altitude, where air pressure held the mercury steady, at

1524 *toises* (a toise was a French unit equal to 1.949 meters); Charles had ascended 6,300 feet. Charles also was first to measure the temperature drop with altitude, called the temperature gradient; it fell from 47° F. on the surface to 11 degrees below zero. Sensing pain in his ears, he clapped on a woolen cap and came down.

The first purely scientific balloon ascension was made July 18, 1803, by Eugene Robertson and a companion named Lhoest, who rose to 23,526 feet over Hamburg, Germany, remaining aloft 5½ hours. They tried numerous experiments with magnetism, and studied the behavior of a "dipping-needle", a device, similar to a magnetic compass, to measure the vertical component of the earth's magnetic lines of force. They discovered something that still bothers airplane pilots today: a magnetic compass needle dips when tilted, causing the compass to behave erratically.

Better prepared to study the atmosphere from a balloon were two French scientists, Joseph Louis Gay-Lussac and Jean B. Biot, who in 1804 were asked by the Academy of Science to measure terrestrial magnetism at great heights. For this mission, they were loaned a French war balloon that had been used in Egypt, outfitted with barometers, thermometers, hygrometers, electrometers, two compasses, a dipping-needle, plus a supply of frogs, insects and birds, to study animal behavior in the high sky. A bee buzzed off in grand style, but a pigeon and a linnet refused to fly away from the balloon. A frog kicked its legs when touched with electric wires from a galvanometer. At a record altitude of 23,012 feet, Gay-Lussac filled two vacuum flasks with air and brought them down for laboratory study. When opened under water, the flasks half filled, showing that atmospheric pressure above 18,000 feet is half sea level pressure, while chemical proportions remain constant. This placed him among the founders of meteorology, with his statement of the relationship of gases in combination, known today as Gay-Lussac's Law.

What did this all mean to balloonists? Aeronauts like John Wise in America were aware of a curious feeling of well-being at high altitudes, but couldn't explain it. Today airmen recognize this as a warning signal of approaching *hypoxia*, or oxygen deficiency. The result is lack of coordination, impaired eyesight, and ultimately loss of consciousness and death.

British meteorologist James Glaisher, a founder of the Aeronautical Society of Great Britain, and his companion, Henry Tracey Coxwell, were the first scientists to encounter hypoxia, recognize it, and return alive to write about it, following an ascent to more than seven miles on September 5, 1862, from Wolverhampton, England.

Soaring high above a stratus cloud deck, Glaisher attempted to photograph the scene, but the balloon was turning too rapidly to permit a time-exposure. Passing through 29,000 feet, he noted the valve-line tangled from the constant rotation. Coxwell climbed into the rigging to reach it, but as Glaisher watched, his vision suddenly became blurred. Glaisher reported:

"I tried to shake myself, but I seemed to have no limbs. In looking at the barometer my head fell over my left shoulder. I struggled and shook my body again, but could not move my arms. I fell backward against the side of the car, resting on the edge. I dimly saw Mr. Coxwell and endeavored to speak, but could not. Darkness overcame me, yet I was still conscious.

"I knew death would come unless we speedily descended. Mr. Coxwell told me later, that while in the ring he felt a piercing cold and his hands were frozen.

James Glaisher and Henry Tracey Coxwell nearly died of hypoxia when their balloon rose above 29,000 feet.

He lost their use, and anxious to open the valve, succeeded in siezing the cord with his teeth and dipping his head two or three times."

Jules Verne's friend, Felix Nadar, had better luck than Glaisher at aerial photography; in 1858 he obtained excellent photographs of Paris. In America, on October 13, 1861, James Wallace Black, a Boston photographer, obtained a good picture of Boston harbor, from the balloon of Samuel A. King, of Philadelphia. The Boston photograph, made on a wet-plate negative, showed square-rigged ships in the harbor and historic buildings that were destroyed in the great fire of 1872. Black's historic negative came into possession of another photographer, W. N. Jennings, of Moylan, Pennsylvania, who provided the print included in this book. Jennings in 1893 took

W. N. Jennings's aerial photograph of Philadelphia—the first made with a yellow filter and ortho plate.

the first aerial photograph using a yellow filter and ortho plate to eliminate haze, showing the heart of Philadelphia.

Regularly scheduled studies of upper winds began in 1893 with the introduction of small unmanned pilot balloons, called *Pibals*, which rise until they burst. Tracked by telescopes to check wind direction and velocity, they were forerunners of modern "Radiosonde" weather balloons, which radio back temperature, pressure, and humidity measurements automatically.

Most remarkable of the weather balloons are stratospheric GHOSTS—an acronym for *G*lobal *HO*rizontal *S*ounding *T*echnique, developed by the National Center for Atmospheric Research, at Boulder, Colorado. GHOSTS were originally conceived in 1958 at the USAF Cambridge Research Laboratories, by Maj. Thomas Haig and Vincent Lally, as a means of utilizing Mylar film and microelectronics in "superpressure" balloons drifting at high altitudes. Completely sealed, the GHOSTS had to be leak-proof. Don Piccard suggested laminating two sheets of Mylar together, to eliminate all pinholes. Partially inflated with helium, the GHOSTS rise and swell until they stabilize, where their total density equals the weight of the displaced air. GHOSTS have circled the globe at 40,000 feet for as long as 351 days.

In the early 1930s Don Piccard's uncle, Auguste Piccard, pioneered manned stratospheric ascents to study cosmic-ray activity. He developed a spherical, pressurized gondola, sponsored by the Belgian Fonds National de la Recherche Scientifique (F.N.R.S.). His balloon dispensed with the traditional netting; the gondola was suspended from a catenary belt around its circumference. When Piccard asked engineers to build his gondola, they said it couldn't be done. All he wanted was

A GHOST balloon of laminated Mylar

a lightweight ball to ride inside, and a window to look out. He solved the problem by asking them to make a spherical beer barrel with windows, so he could look *into* the sphere to check on the fermentation. "But of course!" they replied. "That we can do!"

Throughout the history of aeronautics, brothers have played important roles. There were the brothers Montgolfier, Tissandier, Lilienthal, and Wright. Thus it was not unexpected that Auguste Piccard's twin brother Jean should play an important role in stratospheric ballooning.

For Project *Helios*, Jean Piccard designed a special cabin, from eight spherical triangles joined with straight seams. The result was a spherical octahedron with no "tee" junctures in the seam welds, making them far stronger. The cabin was used three times in Project *Strato Lab.*

Auguste Piccard, with his assistant, Paul Kipfer, made history's first successful flight to the stratosphere, May 27, 1931, from Augsburg, Bavaria, reaching 51,961 feet and coming down on Ober Gurgl glacier in the Austrian Alps. Earlier, in 1927, U. S. Army Capt. Hawthorne C. Gray had penetrated the stratosphere, but was found dead inside his gondola on landing. His barograph had recorded an altitude of 42,470 feet.

As late as 1933 Piccard gondolas were the world's only pressurized aircraft. In 1932 Piccard went up more than ten miles with Max Cosyns, for a new altitude record (53,139 feet). The record returned to the United States November 30, 1933, when T. G. W. Settle of the U. S. Navy and Maj. C. Fordney of the U. S. Marine Corps reached 61,221 feet over New Jersey. During their flight the valve rope escaped from the cabin, and on the way down they had to jettison much of their equipment, even the doors of their gondola.

Three Russian balloonists, Raul F. Fedosienko, A. B. Wasienko, and F. D. Ususkin, headed for the stratosphere from Moscow in 1934 in an 880,000 cubic foot balloon, but died when their cabin broke loose and crashed to earth in a terrifying plunge—their hatch door was bolted shut, trapping them inside. A few months later three American balloonists barely escaped the same fate. Maj. William E. Kepner, Capt. Albert Stevens, and Capt. Orville Anderson went up from Rapid City, South Dakota in *Explorer I*, a monster bag of 3,000,000 cubic feet. Inside their magnesium alloy cabin, the three men rose to 40,000 feet and stabilized there to make cosmic ray studies.

Solar heating caused the hydrogen gas to swell, further inflating the straining gas bag above them. They soon rose above the 60,000-foot level, where the bag suddenly ripped open. Unlike John Wise's deliberate balloon-bursting stunts, this was a catastrophe. The weight of the gondola was too much and they fell earthward, trailing the flapping fabric. Captain Anderson wrenched open the small entry door and hurtled out. Kepner followed, but Stevens somehow got stuck. Kepner, clinging to the outside, shoved him hard with his foot, and at last, with only a few hundred feet of sky left, all three parachutes blossomed as *Explorer I* crashed into a Nebraska field.

That same year, on October 23, Jean Piccard, with his wife Jeannette as pilot, went up through a cloud deck to 57,579 feet altitude, on a cosmic-ray study that took them from Dearborn, Michigan, to Cadiz, Ohio. Jeannette's altitude record on this flight has never been beaten by another woman. And on November 11, 1935, Captains Stevens and Anderson went up again in *Explorer II*, a helium balloon that established a new altitude record of 72,377 feet. It stood for twenty-one years.

This photograph was taken on October 23, 1934, minutes before Jean and Jeannette Piccard, in a pressurized gondola, launched their record-breaking ascent.

In 1936 Jean Piccard had built an unmanned cosmic-ray research balloon from cellophane and scotch tape, and, when new tough, light plastics were developed during World War II, he decided to build a manned plastic balloon, to test a new multiple-balloon theory.

Piccard figured out an engineering riddle. Eight small balloons, each one-half the diameter of a large balloon, would have the same total volume and gross lift as the large one. Yet each small balloon must only weigh one-sixteenth to have the same skin stress. The result—eight little balloons with the same lift would weigh only half as much as the big one! He hooked up ninety-eight sounding balloons in a cluster, like a toy-balloon salesman and made a test hop to 10,000 feet over Rochester, Minnesota. When he wanted to come down, he simply hauled in the balloons one at a time and stuck them with a knife.

In 1946 Piccard launched Project *Helios*, using 80 polyethylene balloons of 250,000 cubic feet each in an effort to ascend to 100,000 feet, but his sponsors, the Navy and General Mills, Inc., decided it wouldn't work. Eleven years later Jean Piccard's son, Don, revived his father's multiple-balloon idea and successfully flew beneath a dozen plastic bags shaped like milk bottles on a two-hour hop from Lancaster, Pennsylvania.

When one balloon burst in the middle of the cluster, Don was amused to see it wriggling through the others "like a runt suckling being pushed away from a sow by his brothers." He pulled down on deflating ropes that forced gas from the bottom of the others and descended safely.

In that same year, on June 2, 1957, it was time for man to explore the stratosphere still higher than Auguste Piccard and Paul Kipher had ascended. Air Force Capt.

Joseph W. Kittinger, Jr. made the ascent in a sealed gondola, supported by a two-million cubic foot plastic balloon. The project balloon, *Man High I*, reached 96,000 feet.

In 1959 Capt. Kittinger launched Project *Excelsior*, a series of remarkable parachute leaps from balloons at the very edge of space. On his first trip he rode his gondola to 76,000 feet and "took a small, ludicrous short hop." He fell spread-eagled, faster and faster, reaching a terminal velocity of 423 miles an hour, then tumbled into a flat spin that blacked him out. The 'chute opened automatically and he landed safely.

On the afternoon of August 16, 1960, Captain Kittinger rode a 360-foot plastic balloon from near Holloman Air Force Base, New Mexico, to 102,800 feet. He stepped out into the void and fell backwards, looking straight up at the balloon, "a beautiful balloon in a beautiful black sky—I had the sensation of lying still, while the balloon raced away from me." His main 'chute deployed safely at 17,500 feet and the rest of the trip was uneventful. For his courage Captain Kittinger won the coveted Harmon Trophy.

The upper limits of manned balloon flight had not been reached, however. One day the following year two stratospheric explorers, Navy Comdr. Malcolm D. Ross and Lt. Comdr. Victor A. Prather, entered a gondola suspended beneath a huge plastic balloon, *Strato-Lab High*, tethered to the deck of the carrier *Antietam*. Before dawn they were on their way to the blackness of the high sky over the Gulf of Mexico, to a record 113,733 feet.

On August 16, 1960, Capt. Joseph W. Kittinger, Jr. jumped from a balloon at an altitude of 102,800 feet and fell more than sixteen miles before opening his parachute.

1968

A. EARLY EGYPTIAN GOOSE I AEROSTAT

1969

B. EGYPTIAN GOOSE II AEROSTAT

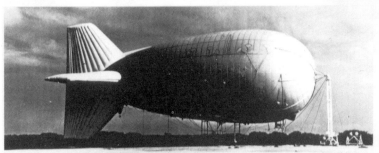

1971

C. ARPA FAMILY II AEROSTAT (S/N 201)

All went well during the descent, until the recovery operation following splashdown. Prather grabbed for a sling lowered from a hovering helicopter and missed. His heavy space suit dragged him beneath the waves to his death. It was a tragic lesson, one that led to use of Navy frogmen in recovery of future space capsules that would take men to the moon and back.

Still higher soared a daring parachutist, Nick Piantandia. On February 2, 1966, he rose from Estherville, Iowa, planning to beat Captain Kittinger's record leap by bailing out at 120,000 feet. He finally reached an unofficial record height of 123,500 feet, found his oxygen system frozen, and came down.

How high can balloons go?

There never will be a balloon that can reach the moon, as Edgar Allan Poe's fictional aeronaut Hans Pfall did using a mysterious gas thirty-seven times lighter than hydrogen, in perhaps Poe's farthest-out tale of mystery and imagination! However, on October 27, 1972, the world's largest research balloon set an unofficial altitude record of 170,000 feet (nearly thirty-two miles).

Developed by the USAF's Cambridge Research Laboratories, the monster 47,800,000 cubic foot balloon, made of extremely thin polyethylene, one-tenth the thickness of writing paper, carried a 250-pound scientific payload.

Not all modern scientific balloons are designed for high-altitude work. Others have been developed for use as stationary tethered aerial platforms for a variety of uses, anchored like kites about two miles above the ground. In the mid-1960s, the Pentagon's Advanced Research Projects Agency (ARPA) experimented with a British World War II barrage balloon, in a project colorfully labeled Egyptian Goose.

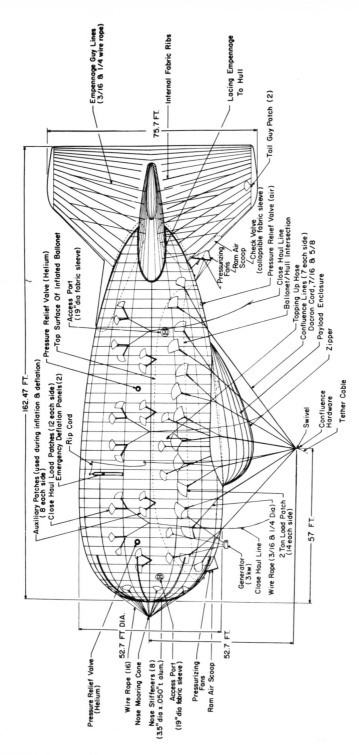

Pressure Relief Valve (Helium)

Empennage Guy Lines (3/16 & 1/4 wire rope)

Internal Fabric Ribs

Lacing Empennage To Hull

75.7 FT.

Tail Guy Patch (2)

162.47 FT.

Auxiliary Patches (used during inflation & deflation) (8 each side)

Pressure Relief Valve (Helium)

Top Surface Of Inflated Ballonet

Access Port (19" dia fabric sleeve)

Close Haul Load Patches (12 each side)

Emergency Deflation Panels (2)

Rip Cord

Pressurizing Fans

Ram Air Scoop

Pressure Relief Valve (air)

Check Valve (collapsible fabric sleeve)

Close Haul Line

Ballonet/Hull Intersection

Topping Up Hose

Confluence Lines (7 each side)

Dacron Cord, 7/16 & 5/8

Payload Enclosure

Zipper

Swivel

Confluence Hardware

Tether Cable

52.7 FT. DIA.

Wire Rope (16)

Nose Mooring Cone

Nose Stiffeners (8) (3.5" dia x .050" t alum.)

Access Port (19" dia fabric sleeve)

Pressurizing Fans

Ram Air Scoop

Pressure Relief Valve (Helium)

Generator (3 kw)

Close Haul Line

Wire Rope (3/16 & 1/4 Dia)

2 Ton Load Patch (14 each side)

57 FT.

52.7 FT.

FAMILY II TETHERED BALLOON, GENERAL ARRANGEMENT
200,000 CUBIC FOOT

Under a ARPA contract, the G. T. Schjeldahl Company of Northfield, Minnesota, developed from Egyptian Goose a huge, 250,000 cubic-foot Family II Aerostat, whose hull and tail fins stay bloated under continuous pressurization. This provides better streamlining, to help it ride out gale winds up to 70 mph. Such aerostats, made from laminated fabric and plastic and inflated with helium, can lift payloads of 3,500 pounds to 10,000 feet, to serve as television relay stations, communications platforms, weather stations, or military surveillance outposts, much as balloons were first used in warfare in 1794.

Balloons have carried planetary spacecraft, such as the Mars Viking lander, high in the sky for drop tests, and there have been proposals to use balloons to lower such sophisticated craft to the Red Planet. No end appears in sight for these simple and wonderful globes that opened the way to man's conquest of the sky two centuries ago.

12

HANDS OFF!

Who is the world hot-air ballooning champion? This was what 128 balloonists wanted to find out in February, 1973, when they assembled at Albuquerque, New Mexico, to compete in the First World Hot-Air Balloon Championship meet. Organizer of the unusual event was Bob Waligunda, a director of the Balloon Federation of America and International Professional Balloon Pilots Racing Association. Like the other aerial sports of sky diving, soaring, and sports-plane flying, hot-air ballooning has developed a loosely-knit group of regular participants seeking an identity, and, like the heavier-than-air Professional Race Pilots Association, the lighter-than-air group solicits sponsorships to make championship meets work.

Balloons and dirigibles have been used in aerial advertising since the turn of the century, when John Knox, of Johnstown, New York, painted the letters G-E-L-A-T-I-N-E on the side of a dirigible that appeared at the St. Louis World's Fair in 1905. Today you'll find balloons in the shape of beer cans, balloons with flashing neon signs, and balloons gaily decorated with flags and bunting, just as they were in the days of the Montgolfiers. Showmanship has always been an important part of ballooning.

At Albuquerque, pride and prejudice were put aside, everybody did their best to have a good time, and the results were grand. To determine who was the world's greatest hot-air balloonist, special events were held—a rapid-climb and level-off test, a climbing-and-descending flight-control test, and a spot-landing test. Winner

Balloonists assembled in Albuquerque, New Mexico, to compete in the First World Hot-Air Balloon Championship meet.

Don Piccard's *Spirit of '76* in flight

was Dennis Floden, who runs a balloon enterprise, American Aeropromotion, at Flint, Michigan. Second was Bill Cutter of Phoenix, Arizona, and third was Janne Balkedal of Sweden. The big day was the finale, when 126 balloons soared into the blue New Mexico sky at the same time, a dazzling spectacle.

As a result of such energetic effort, hot-air ballooning is becoming recognized as a sport for everyone, not just the wealthy. Regional ballooning meets are now scheduled frequently throughout the nation and abroad. Typical was one at Albuquerque in 1972, where the traditional Hare-and-Hound Race was colorfully called the "Roadrunner and Coyote Race."

In this enjoyable event, Sid Cutter's Roadrunner balloon lifted off at 7:45 in the morning, with the Coyote balloons following fifteen minutes later at thirty-second intervals. Matt Wiederkehr, holder of the hot-air balloon long distance record of 196.71 miles, chased the Roadrunner in a Raven AX-6, *Flying Raven I*, and landed nearby for an early lead. Next, Don Piccard's wife, Wilma, maneuvered her Piccard AX-6 *Gypsy* to within 206 feet of the Roadrunner for first place. Then her husband, Don, leaped off in his handsome *Spirit of '76*, a Piccard AX-8, and landed twenty-two feet closer for an exciting one-two finish.

To Don Piccard, hot-air ballooning is truly the "Sport of the Seventies." He elaborates: "The aeronaut will always be that special person who can realize real beauty from basic, simple, and clear functions of time and space, not requiring complicated artificial gadgetry to salve his sensations. The true greatness in the balloon lies in its basic simplicity in design and function, balanced against the unending variations of the environment."

The start of a balloon race at Reno, Nevada

One hot-air balloon enthusiast, Bill Berry, president of the Hot Air Balloon Club of America in Concord, California, switched from sky-diving after a knee injury, when a friend invited him to "try going up instead of coming down." Right away he became a "balloonatic" and has since logged more than 1500 hours in hot-air balloons. Berry, an FAA balloonist examiner, enjoys "walking" a balloon across puffy cumulus clouds, touching the top of each with his gondola. The majority of balloonists going through his school are airline pilots seeking new recreation in cloudland.

At the National Air Races in Reno, Nevada, in 1965, Berry had an experience that still gives him nightmares. Rising into the clear sky, he thought he heard a muffled shout above the roar of his propane burners, but could see no other balloon nearby. He shrugged it off. At 3,000 feet, when he shut down the burners, a young voice cried: "Please, mister, won't you get me down?" Dangling at the end of a ground line, hanging from the side of the balloon too far out to reach, was eleven-year-old Danny Nowell, whose arm had somehow gotten tangled in the line. Berry talked fast, telling Danny not to look down, that everything would be alright. He brought the balloon down carefully, and Danny lived to tell about his narrow escape.

Essentially, ballooning is a safe sport when the rules are followed. Over a decade the only recorded fatalities, according to government records, were three persons lost at sea in an unsuccessful effort to cross the Atlantic with an untested device.

Much of learning to operate a hot-air balloon has to do with safety, just as in learning to fly an airplane. Until a few years ago, all you needed to get a balloon pilot's license was to walk into the nearest FAA General Aviation District Office and tell them you wanted one—they

A ballooning student gets ready to go aloft for flying instruction.

simply wrote it out and handed it to you. Today things are different, yet becoming a licensed balloonist is not difficult. It takes roughly eight to ten hours of flying, plus ground school. To become a student balloon pilot, you must be at least sixteen years old, and before you can solo you must be seventeen and hold a Third Class Medical Certificate.

There are now a number of ballooning schools in the United States. To locate the one nearest you, drop a line to the Balloon Federation of America, Suite 610, 806 Fifteenth Street, N.W., Washington, D.C. 20005.

There are also many licensed commercial balloon pilots who can legally give instruction in ballooning, but because qualifying for such a license is relatively easy, use caution. As Don Piccard points out, four people could go up in a balloon over a desert dry lake, float there eight hours, reach 5,000 feet at one point, come down and bounce the gondola eight times on the ground, and all four could automatically qualify for commercial balloonist licenses!

The cost of learning to balloon is rather high, around $1,000, although some club rates are lower. Some ballooning clubs offer part ownership of their balloons. Recently, the FAA began issuing approval certificates to schools, and information on these can be obtained from your nearest FAA General Aviation District Office.

In a typical curriculum, you'll be introduced to rigid safety procedures and participate in the loading, transportation, unloading, and inflation of the balloon, including layout, equipment assembly, and operation of the propane burner. Your instructor will introduce you to principles of lighter-than-air flight in a ground school session. After a tethered flight (really more difficult than free flight), you'll be given an orientation free flight, learn how to maintain level flight, descend, and stow the balloon.

On the second flight, you'll learn more about your equipment—gondola, envelope, fuel tanks and burner, flight instruments, and ground inflation procedures. You'll practice more ascents in both tethered and free flight, experience a "flameout" of the burner, and learn how to relight it. In ground school you'll study load limits, temperature limits, and what documents you must carry

A careful balloonist periodically checks the interior of his balloon.

in flight—an Operator's Manual, Certificate of Airworthiness, and Aircraft Registration, plus your own medical certificate, which is your student permit.

Safety procedures occupy much of your third hour—how to fill propane tanks properly, how to detect leaks, what to do in emergency situations such as an on-board fire. Then more work on flameout and relight procedures, plus precise control of ascent and descent accelerations. Ground school studies will include some meteorology, duties of the ground crew, and safe operation of your balloon near power lines or open water.

The fourth flight gets you deeper into emergency situations, navigation, and dangerous weather situations to avoid. You'll learn to drift along ground contours, and how to deflate the balloon just prior to landing. Ground school subjects will include chart-reading, selecting emergency landing areas, water landings, and handling the balloon in strong thermal activity.

On your fifth flight, you should be ready to handle the entire journey on your own. If your instructor thinks you're ready, you'll be allowed to ascend alone on a tethered flight, level off, and come down. More work now comes in ground school on handling your balloon in gusty air, preparation for high-altitude flight, and proper landing after a rapid descent.

Your sixth flight will be still more exciting, for now you're ready to drift cross-country in command of your balloon. Your instructor will be along, pointing out pertinent things from the FAA's Part 91 General Operating and Flight Rules that govern all air traffic. (Balloons have the right of way over airplanes, gliders, and helicopters, but the wise balloonist won't insist on it!)

On this flight you'll learn to use the radio for communications, such as advising ground controllers if you

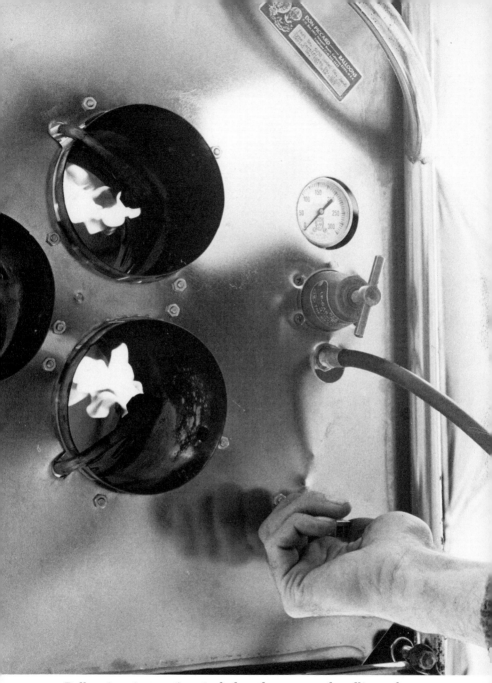

Ballooning instruction includes the proper handling of propane tanks.

Few experiences rival the excitement of hot-air ballooning.

should enter specific air traffic zones. In ground school, refined climb and descent techniques will be reviewed, along with use of venting on landing, and landing with burner only.

The seventh flight gets you into advanced ballooning on hot days when the air is thin, and takeoffs and landings in and out of small fields. Principles of high-altitude flight are studied in class, along with cloud flying and a review of the fuel system operation, with the stress on safety.

Your eighth flight takes you up to 5,000 feet with your instructor, who will permit you to practice more solo flying, while on the ground you'll bone up for the FAA written examination (forty questions). And you'll review any subject material necessary to qualify you for the FAA flight check, which may be given by an FAA representative.

Should you wish to apply for an "unlimited free ballooning" rating, you must make at least one ascent to 10,000 feet, and pass a written examination of fifty questions on weather, navigation, FAA regulations, and balloon operating procedures. The passing score on both hot-air and unlimited ratings is 70 percent.

The great day finally comes, when you can soar away confidently to ride the winds with the ghosts of the Montgolfiers and those who have discovered ballooning since then. Whether you join a balloon club or buy or make your own balloon, you'll be proud to belong to a growing fraternity of enthusiasts of the most glorious of all aerial sports, hot-air ballooning!

CHRONOLOGY

1783, June 5   Joseph and Etienne Montgolfier send paper hot-air balloon up 6,000 feet over Annonay, France.

1783, August 26   First hydrogen balloon ascent in Paris.

1783, September 19   Sheep, cock, and duck ascend in a Montgolfier from Versailles.

1783, October 15   Pilatre de Rozier makes tethered ascent.

1783, November 21   Girond de Villette makes tethered ascent.

1783, November 21   Rozier and the Marquis d'Arlandes make first free balloon flight.

1783, December 1   Messieurs Charles and Robert ascend in hydrogen balloon.

1784, April 4   George Washington predicts transatlantic ballooning.

1784, May 10   First hot-air paper balloon ascent in America.

1784, June 25   Edward Warren, thirteen, makes first tethered ascent in America.

1784, September 24   Vincent Lunardi first to ascend from England.

1785, January 7   Dr. John Jeffries and Jean-Pierre Blanchard cross English Channel by balloon.

1785, July 11   Hot-air balloon carries dummy up over Puebla, Mexico, during fiesta.

1793, January 9   Blanchard makes first free ascent in America.

1794, April 2   First military balloon school formed at Meudon, France.

1794, June 2   First combat reconnaissance operation from a balloon, Mauberge, France.

1803, July 18   Eugene Robertson makes first ascent for science.

1804, September 15   Gay-Lussac and Biot determine composition of upper atmosphere.

1804, December 11   Napoleon's coronation announced by balloon.

1817, July 6   Madame Blanchard dies in balloon tragedy.

1825, July 9   Robertson makes first ascent from New York.

1825, October 18   Madame Johnson is first woman balloonist in America.

1825, October 31   Horse-balloon patent granted to Citizen Genet.

1830, September 10   Charles Durant becomes first American aeronaut.

1835, May 2   John Wise makes first ascent.

1836, November 7   Charles Green pilots Vauxhall balloon 480 miles from London to Germany.

1842, March 29   John Pennington's Steam Balloon proposal studied in U. S. Senate.

1844, April 13   New York *Sun* prints Edgar Allan Poe's balloon hoax.

1847   Smithsonian telegraph weather-reporting system established.

1847, December   Rufus Porter flies six-foot dirigible model in a New York auditorium.

1852, September 24   Henri Giffard flies 140-foot dirigible 6 mph under steam power.

1858, October 23   Felix Nadar takes first aerial photographs from a balloon over Paris.

1859, July 1   John Wise's balloon *Atlantic* travels 1200 miles from St. Louis to Henderson, N. Y.

1861, April 19   Professor T. S. C. Lowe, Yankee balloonist, is captured by Rebels, first prisoner of Civil War.

1861, April   John Starkweather operates balloon from the vessel Mayflower in South Carolina—the first "aircraft carrier."

1861, June 18   Lowe sends first telegram from a balloon, to Abraham Lincoln.

1861, October 13   James Wallace Black takes first aerial photos in America, from balloon over Boston.

1862, May 29   Professor Lowe becomes "most-shot-at man in the Civil War" at Battle of Fair Oaks.

1862, September 5   Glashier and Coxwell suffer from hypoxia at 37,000 feet.

1863   Count Ferdinand von Zeppelin makes first balloon ascent, from Fort Snelling, Minnesota.

1863, July 4   Confederate balloon captured by Yanks.

1863, October 18   Nadar's balloon *Le Géant* drifts from Paris to Hanover, Germany.

1864, July 5   Solomon Andrews patents *Aereon* dirigible, organizes first chartered U.S. airline.

1866, May 25   Andrews carries three passengers over New York City in his *Aereon* dirigible.

1870–71   Balloons used to lift the Siege of Paris; 2,500,000 air mail letters posted.

1878, June 12   Charles Ritchel patents one-man dirigible, flies it over Hartford, Conn.

1883, October 8   Albert and Gaston Tissandier fly 92-foot electric-powered dirigible, Auteuil, France.

1884, August 9   A. C. Krebs, Charles Renard fly 165-foot electric dirigible.

1897, July 11   Salomon Andree North Pole expedition vanishes, found thirty-three years later.

1898, June 30   Sgt. Ivy Baldwin, U.S. Signal Corps, observes Spanish-American War from balloon over Cuba.

1898, September 20   Alberto Santos-Dumont flies first gasoline-powered dirigible.

1900, July 2   LZ-1, first Zeppelin dirigible, flies near Lake Constance.

1901, October 19   Santos-Dumont circles Eiffel Tower in dirigible to win 100,000-franc French Aero club's prize.

1905   Dirigible *Gelatine* is first used for aerial advertising, St. Louis World's Fair.

1906, September 6   Frank P. Lahm wins first James Gordon Bennett balloon race.

1909, August 29   Zeppelin begins scheduled passenger service with dirigibles in Europe.

1910, October 15   Walter Wellman fails to cross Atlantic by dirigible.

1912, July   Privately-owned dirigible *Akron* burns over Atlantic City, N. J.

1919, July 2–6   British airship R-34 is first to cross Atlantic.

1922, *February* 21   America's first big semi-rigid airship, the Italian-built *Roma*, destroyed by fire.

1924, *October*   Dirigible LZ-126 *Los Angeles* crosses Atlantic.

1925, *September* 3   Dirigible *Shenandoah* lost in storm over Ohio.

1928, *May* 24   Airship *Italia* crashes in Arctic.

1930, *October* 5   British dirigible R-101 crashes in France.

1931, *May* 27   Auguste Piccard reaches the stratosphere by balloon.

1933, *April* 4   Dirigible *Akron* crashes.

1933, *November* 30   Settle and Fordney set altitude record in stratospheric balloon at 61,221 feet.

1934, *January* 30   Three Russian balloonists die when gondola breaks loose.

1934, *July* 27   Stratosphere balloon *Explorer I* crashes.

1935, *February* 12   Dirigible *Macon* wrecked off California coast.

1935, *November* 11   *Explorer II* reaches 72,377 feet.

1936, *May* 6   Dirigible *Hindenburg* inaugurates regular transatlantic passenger service.

1936, *June* 24   Jean Piccard builds balloon of cellophane and scotch tape.

1937, *May* 6   Hindenburg burns.

1946–47   Jean Piccard attempts to build multiple-balloon for stratospheric flight—Project Helios.

1947, *February* 16   Don Piccard makes first postwar ascent in United States.

1958, *December* 12   Balloon *Free World* attempts Atlantic crossing east to west.

1960, *August* 16   Capt. Joseph W. Kittinger, Jr. reaches 102,800 feet in balloon, bails out.

1960   Ed Yost ascends to 9,300 feet in first successful modern hot-air balloon.

1961   Balloonists Ross and Prather balloon to 113,733 feet. Prather drowns on splashdown.

1961, *July* 19   Don Piccard sets five world records in one flight with balloon *Golden Bear*.

1966, *February* 2   Balloonist Nick Piantandia reaches 123,500 feet.

1966, September 12   Tracy Barnes completes first transcontinental hot-air balloon flight five months after start.

1970, September 21   Transatlantic balloon *Free Life* lost at sea with three aboard.

1972, March 29   Matt Wiederkehr sets hot-air balloon record of 196.71 miles distance, 8 hours 48 minutes duration.

1972, July 14   Julian Mott reaches 36,000 feet in hot-air balloon.

1972, October 10   Cambridge Research Laboratories research balloon reaches 170,000 feet altitude.

1973, February 11–17   World's first International Hot-Air Balloon Championship meet, Albuquerque, N. M.

BALLOON MAKERS

The largest manufacturer of hot-air balloons in the world is Raven Industries, Inc., Box 1007, Sioux Falls, South Dakota 57101; telephone, 605–336–2750. Raven balloons are FAA Type Certificated and carry Standard Airworthiness Certificates. They range in size and price from the one-man beginner's Model S-40A ($4,125) to the king-size S-60AC ($11,900). Most popular is the S-50A, normally rated for two persons.

The S-50A is equipped with: A fifty-foot diameter high tenacity nylon envelope, volume 56,400 cu. ft. Deflation panel and maneuvering vent. Dual stainless steel burner with 4,000,000 Btu/hr. maximum output. Three ten-gallon aluminum propane tanks with gauges. Lightweight aluminum frame gondola with resilient fiberglass insert. Quick detach instrument panel with standard aircraft altimeter, rate-of-climb, free air temperature gauge, and magnetic compass. The price is $5,495.

The second largest hot-air balloon maker is Don Piccard, P. O. Box 1902, Newport Beach, California 92663; telephone, 714–642–3545. Piccard balloons are FAA Type Certificated and carry Standard Airworthiness Certificates. Most popular is the Piccard AX-6 three-man balloon, which sells for $5,000 F.O.B. Newport Beach.

The AX-6 Piccard envelope is 506 feet in diameter, made of 1.2-ounce rip-stop nylon, acrylic treated to reduce porosity. It consists of twelve gores of twenty-six panels each with twelve 4000-pound test tubular nylon load tapes, blank equator panel cooling vent, and straight seam Velcro rip panel deflation system. Two ten-gallon aluminum fuel tanks feed propane to pressure-regulated blast valves with a separate vapor-system pilot control. The basket is 36" x 48" x 40" of Borneo rattan wickerwork with reinforced stainless steel cable, ¾" marine mahogany plywood floor, and hemp carrying handles. Instruments include a Weston 6" direct reading apex pyrometer 50-300 degrees, fuel pressure gauge, compass, altimeter, and rate-of-climb gauge.

The third largest manufacturer of hot-air balloons is Mark Semich, of SEMCO Balloons, 2002 N. 11th St. Couer D'Alene, Idaho 83814; telephone, 208–664–2220. In addition there are a number of individual balloon makers here and abroad; their names are available from the Balloon Federation of America, Suite 610, 806 Fifteenth Street, N.W., Washington, D.C. 20005.

BALLOON SCHOOLS

The Federal Aviation Administration's General Aviation District Offices (GADOs) will supply the name of the flight schools and ground schools nearest you where ballooning courses are available. Any licensed commercial balloon pilot can give ballooning instruction. Among the more active:

Bob Waligunda, Balloon Enterprises, Inc., Box 102, Forest Park Station, Springfield, Massachusetts 01108; telephone, 413–739–6276. Waligunda operates four balloon schools, the newest at Kobelt Airport, Wallkill, N. Y. 12589, telephone 914–895–2016, ask for Bill Hughes.

Jim Knight, Balloon Ascensions, Ltd., Route 11, Box 279, Statesville, North Carolina 28677; telephone, 704–872–4277. An ex-USAF Captain, Knight joined balloonist Bill Meadows to form one of the largest flight training balloon centers in the nation. The firm has four instructors and represents Piccard Balloons in twenty-six states.

Bruce Comstock, Aerostatica, Inc., 1742 Traver Road, Ann Arbor, Michigan 48105; telephone, 313–769–3668. Comstock, editor of Ballooning Magazine, offers training in Piccard AX-6 and Raven S-50A hot-air balloons.

Other instructors are:
Bill Berry, 3300 Orchard Avenue, Concord, California 94520; telephone, 415–682–3168.
Chauncey M. Dunn, 4643 Wadsworth, Denver, Colorado 80033; telephone, 303–422–1471.

Matt Wiederkehr, Minnesota Balloon School, 1604 Euclid
Street, St. Paul, Minnesota 55106; telephone, 612–774–
5208.
Dennis Floden, American Aeropromotion, P. O. Box 3039,
Flint, Michigan 48502; telephone, 313–629–5549.
Derek Howard, 1403 Meriden Lane, Austin, Texas 78703;
telephone, 512–478–4059.
Jerry Melsha, P. O. Box 932, Sioux Falls, South Dakota
57101; telephone, 605–743–2771.
W. R. Walden, 1834 Main Street, Sarasota, Florida 23577;
telephone, 813–955–4191.
John Ross, 630 Sherbrooke Street, Montreal 11, Quebec,
Canada.

BALLOON CLUBS
AND SOCIETIES

Balloon Federation of America, Suite 610, 806 Fifteenth
Street, N.W., Washington, D. C. 20005.
Lighter-Than-Air Society, 1800 Triplett Boulevard, Akron,
Ohio 44306.
Aerostat Society of Minnesota, 310 Cedar Street, St. Paul,
Minnesota 55101.
Free Balloon Pilot's Society, 333 Southgate Drive, North-
brook, Illinois 60002.
Balloonatics Balloon Club, 2345 Walnut Street, Denver, Colo-
rado 80205.
Cleveland Balloon Club, 1225 Euclid Avenue, Cleveland,
Ohio 44115.
L.E.R.C. Wind Drifters, 2814 Empire Avenue, Burbank, Cali-
fornia 91503.
Calgary Balloon Club, 1712 Home Road N.W., Calgary 45,
Alberta, Canada.

International Alpine Balloon Society, Gotthardstreasse 5a, 8800 THALWIL, Switzerland.
British Balloon & Airship Club, Artillery Mansions, 75 Victoria Street, London SW 1, England.
London Balloon Club, 10 Ardross Avenue, Northwood, Middlesex, England.
Cambridge Balloon Club, 344 Wanstead Park Road, Cranbrook, Ilford, Essex, England.
Irish Balloon Club, 50 Mountjoy Square, Dublin 1, Eire.

BIBLIOGRAPHY

American Heritage. *The American Heritage History of Flight.* New York: Simon & Schuster, 1962.

Amik, M. L. *History of Donaldson's Balloon Ascensions.* Cincinnati: Cincinnati News Co., 1875.

Dolfus, Charles, & Henri Bouche. *Histoire de l'Aeronautique.* Paris: L'Illustration, 1932.

Hastings, George Everett. *The Life and Work of Francis Hopkinson.* Chicago: The University of Chicago Press, 1926.

Hodgson, J. F. *The History of Aeronautics in Great Britain.* London: Oxford University Press, 1924.

LERC Balloon Club. *Ballooning Training Manuals.* Burbank, Calif.: LERC Wind Drifters, 2814 Empire Ave., n.d.

Marion, F. *Wonderful Balloon Ascents.* London: Cassell, Petter & Galpin, 1870.

Miller, Francis Trevelyan. *The World In The Air.* New York: G. P. Putnam's Sons, 1930.

Piccard, Joan Russell. *Adventure On The Wind.* Los Angeles: Nash Publishing Company, 1971.

Sparks, Jared. *The Life Of George Washington.* Boston: Little, Brown & Co., 1854.

Turnor, Hatton. *Astra Castra, Experiments and Adventures in the Atmosphere.* London: Chapman & Hall, 1865.

Wise, John. *Through The Air.* Philadelphia: To-Day Printing and Publishing Company, 1873.

INDEX

177